HOW TO GET GRANTS AND GIFTS FOR THE PUBLIC SCHOOLS

HOW TO GET GRANTS AND GIFTS FOR THE PUBLIC SCHOOLS

Stanley Levenson

Allyn and Bacon
Boston • London • Toronto • Sydney • Tokyo • Singapore

Series Editor: Arnis E. Burvikovs
Series Editorial Assistant: Matthew Forster
Executive Marketing Manager: Stephen Smith
Editorial-Production Administrator: Beth Houston
Editorial-Production Service: Walsh & Associates, Inc.
Composition Buyer: Linda Cox
Manufacturing Buyer: Julie McNeill
Cover Administrator: Kristina Mose-Libon

Library of Congress Cataloging-in-Publication Data
Levenson, Stanley.
    How to get grants and gifts for the public schools / Stanley Levenson.
        p.   cm.
    Includes bibliographical references (p.) and index.
    ISBN 0-205-30887-2
    1. Educational fund raising—United States.   2. Proposal writing for grants—United States.   3. Education—United States—Finance.
I. Title.

LC243 .L49 2001
379.1'2—dc21

                                                                      2001046314

Printed in the United States of America

10 9 8 7 6 5 4 3 2 1   04 03 02 01

To Kay, Carla, Mark, and Al, my best friends

Contents

Preface

There is a critical need for increased funding to the public schools. The tax base, just like the tax base for state colleges and universities, is not enough to provide a "world-class" education for all our children. Schools need additional funding for new and innovative program offerings, including programs in the arts, mathematics, sciences, English, and foreign languages. Monies are needed for new technology, including computers, printers, scanners, and software. Teachers need additional staff development to keep them up to date with changing curriculum and changing technology. Budgets are already strained paying for competitive teacher salaries and fringe benefits, hiring additional staff, maintaining buildings and grounds, acquiring land, building and wiring new facilities, and remodeling existing ones.

While the public schools have been struggling to meet the needs of all the children, private schools, colleges, universities, and nonprofit organizations have been busy raising billions of dollars each year by tapping into corporations, foundations—and most important, private citizens—for large grants and gifts utilizing sophisticated, "tried-and-true" techniques taught in workshops and courses all over the country. Public schools must look beyond their traditional external funding sources if they are to stay competitive. Sitting idly by while private schools and others reap all the rewards is no longer an option.

Every day of every year people are giving to good causes. Public education is obviously a good cause. The schools have such great potential to raise serious money. All they have to do is find out how, and ask! Instead of concentrating on bake sales, car washes, pizza sales, gift wrap sales, and other "nickel-and-dime" fundraising efforts, teachers, administrators, school board members, and parents should be seeking more lucrative ways of raising major dollars for the schools. These ways are descibed in this book.

To address the overall fundraising needs, desires, and capacity of the public schools to raise monies and compete with other entities on equal footing, a number of communities across the nation have formed Local Education Foundations (LEFs). These foundations employ executive directors, consultants, grantwriters, and other full-time staff to coordinate a comprehensive fundraising effort. By communicating their schools' needs to their constituency and to corporations and foundations, some school districts and consortia of districts are beginning to reap major rewards. Recently, Walter Annenberg gave $500 million to bring about systemic change in large urban schools systems, rural school systems, and arts education programs. The Bill and Melinda Gates Foundation gave a $350 million gift aimed at improving our nation's schools, including a $56 million gift to support the design and development of small schools. Former Netscape CEO Jim Barksdale and his wife Sally created a $100 million endowment to advance literacy in his home state of Mississippi. Former Wal-Mart Corporation president Ferold Arend and his wife Jane made a gift of $5 million to build an art center at Bentonville High School in Bentonville, Arkansas, and his colleague Jack Shewmaker and his family added an additional $1 million to equip the center. These generous individuals, many of whom attended public schools, are committed to helping schools survive and prosper.

The focus of this book is to show you how to tap into the vast array of funding sources that are out there for the asking. The book offers many worthwhile suggestions and techniques that will make you more competitive in your search for corporate, foundation, and government grants and in your pursuit of gifts from individual members of your community. Throughout the book you will find many World Wide Web addresses that will save you much time and make you more competitive. Chapter 1, Applying for Government Grants, concentrates on the many types of government grants available, including discretionary grants and formula grants. You will learn that government grants are very competitive and difficult to obtain. You will identify the most common mistakes grantseekers make that can cost you when applying for a government grant and five secrets of successful grantseekers. The book will provide you with the names and website addresses of major government funding agencies. At the conclusion of this chapter you will be prepared to write and compete for a government grant.

In Chapter 2, Applying for Corporate and Foundation Grants, you will learn that there are hundreds of grant opportunities out there for the asking. You will become familiar with corporate and foundation grants and why they may be easier to obtain than government grants. You will discover the impact of corporate and foundation giving, and learn strategies for winning funding for pre-K–12 schools. Finally, you will learn how to do prospect research using the World Wide Web and the names of 29 corporations and foundations that regularly give grants and gifts to the public schools.

Chapter 3 focuses on individual solicitation and the public schools. In this chapter you will learn the significance and impact of individual giving in the United States, including the fact that more than 82 percent of all external funding comes from individuals. You will discover that more than $150 billion was contributed by individuals and bequests as the twentieth century ended. Also included in this chapter are suggestions for setting up a Local Education Foundation, an explanation of the differences between annual campaigns and capital campaigns and a fourteen-step approach to individual solicitation of grants and gifts. Finally, a clear-cut discussion of planned giving is presented that not only defines what planned giving is, but also offers a list of noncash gifts that might be donated to the schools such as appreciated marketable securities, entire interest in real estate, remainder interest in real property, tangible personal property and life insurance proceeds.

In Chapters 4 and 5, How to Write a Grant Application, Parts I and II, you will learn the differences between writing a government grant application and writing a corporate and foundation grant application. You will practice writing the six basic components of a grant application, including needs assessment documentation, goals, objectives, activities, evaluation specifications, and budget, and learn to put together a dissemination plan and a project summary. You will learn helpful hints to improve your chances of getting funded. Finally, you will learn to write a mini-grant using a sample mini-grant application provided in the book.

Copies of successful grant applications appear in Chapters 6 and 7. These applications represent both large and small grants. The applications provide valuable insight into what a successful grant application looks like, including grant formatting, writing styles, writing content, and the requirements of various funding agencies. Included in Chapter 6 are two mini-grants, one to the San Diego Foundation, San Diego, California, and the other to the South Washington County Education Foundation, Cottage Grove, Minnesota. Another application, submitted by the National School District, National City, California, to the Alliance Healthcare Foundation, provides an example of what a typical foundation requires for funding. A successful federal grant application, which was submitted by the Sumner County Board of Education, Gallatin, Tennessee, to the 21st Century Community Learning Centers Program of the U.S. Department of Education, is presented in Chapter 7. Chapter 8 focuses on implementation of a fundraising plan at the school or district level and Chapter 9 provides an overall summary of the book. By studying the grantwriting strategies presented in this book and combining them with actual examples of successful applications, you should have all you need to begin to formulate and write your own successful application.

In the appendices you will find the most salient features of a Federal Grant Application (ED 424), a scoring rubric for the 21st Century Community Learning Centers Program, and a sample cover letter for a corporate or foundation grant. A sampling of K-12 grants winners from across the country and their funding agency is also provided, as well as a glossary of terms for both government grants and corporate and foundation grants.

Acknowledgments

Many ideas and examples in this book come from my experience as a classroom teacher and district-level administrator in the public schools, from my work as a fundraising consultant to the schools, and from the classes and workshops I teach for the University of California at San Diego and elsewhere.

I would not be able to write a book like this, however, without a great deal of assistance from students, teachers, principals, volunteers, and others who have participated in my workshops and classes and have offered worthwhile suggestions to make the book practical and usable. Of special note, I would like to thank my wife Kay Pantelis, a true "master teacher" who has encouraged me and kept me motivated and on task; my daughter Carla Levenson for providing extensive assistance with manuscript editing; and my son Mark Levenson for his encouragement and helpful business and marketing suggestions.

I would also like to recognize Carol J. Mitchell, Program Director of the 21st Century Community Learning Centers Program of the U.S. Department of Education, for her invaluable cooperation and assistance. Special thank yous go to Candice Young, who has edited all chapters of the book; Dr. James Retson, Emeritus Professor of Education, San Diego State University, for his invaluable input to the evaluation section of Chapter 5; and Jodi Witte, Grant Coordinator, South Washington County Schools, Cottage Grove, Minnesota, for her kind assistance with Chapter 6. Much appreciation is extended to the following people who have read specific chapters and made valuable suggestions for improvement: Scott Fisher, Bob Greenamyer, Al Marini, and Cliff Underwood. Also, a special thank you to those people and their schools or school districts who have given me permission to reprint their successful applications in the book: Sharon Miller Thompson, Park High School, Cottage Grove, MN; Bob Greenamyer, Park Village Elementary School, Poway Unified School District, Poway, CA; George Cameron, National School District, National City, CA; and Pat Conner, Sumner County Board of Education, Gallatin, TN. Finally, I would like to express my appreciation to Christina and Peter Rothenbach for their assistance with computer graphics, and to Dave Carpenter, one of the finest cartoonists in America, who has helped to liven the book with his keen and creative wit.

Many people at Allyn and Bacon have helped the writing effort and facilitated the publishing of the manuscript. First, if it were not for Sandi Kirshner, President, this book would have never gotten off the ground. My initial conversation with her convinced me to go with Allyn and Bacon because of the depth of her knowledge and understanding of the need for a book like this. To Arnis E. Burvikovs, Series Editor, for his encouragement and kind and gentle manner; to Matthew Forster, my Editorial Assistant, who was always there to answer questions and lend a helping hand, and to Kathy Whittier of Walsh & Associates for handling the nuts and bolts of production for the book. Also, many thanks to the following people who were asked to review the book and made worthwhile and insightful recommendations: Jodi Witte, South Washington County Schools (MN); Samir A. Haddad, Farmington Public Schools (MI); Richard Fluck, Northern Illinois University; David Strom, San Diego State University; and Jan Richards, Farmington Public Schools (MI).

About the Author

Dr. Stan Levenson is a nationally recognized fundraising consultant to the public schools with more than thirty years of experience as a classroom teacher, principal, district-level administrator, university professor, and educational consultant. He has extensive fundraising experience at all grade levels and in all content areas. He has raised more than $40 million in grants and gifts and is responsible for training others who have raised more than $50 million. Dr. Levenson has served as a consultant to more than fifty school districts throughout California as well as in New York, Massachusetts, Nevada, Hawaii, Guam, and Germany. He has written extensively for publication and has trained and assisted hundreds of classroom teachers, principals, district level administrators, parents, and board members to obtain grants and gifts from corporations, foundations, the government, and wealthy individuals. In addition to his work as a fundraising consultant to the schools, Dr. Levenson also teaches fundraising and grantwriting classes for the University of California at San Diego. Dr. Levenson received his bachelor's degree from the State University of New York at Oswego, his master's degree from UCLA, and his doctorate from United States International University in San Diego, California, where he now resides. He can be contacted through his website: *www.grantsandgiftsfor schools.com.*

HOW TO GET GRANTS AND GIFTS FOR THE PUBLIC SCHOOLS

1
Applying for Government Grants

In this chapter you will

❏ Identify types of government grants for pre-K–12 schools

❏ Distinguish between formula grants and discretionary grants

❏ Learn why government grants are difficult to obtain

❏ Understand the financial involvement of the federal government in the grant making process

❏ Identify the many government grant opportunities for pre-K–12

❏ Discover ways to improve your chances of getting funded

❏ Become familiar with a government grant application

❏ Understand how to prepare a Federal Grant Application for funding

❏ Identify the three most common mistakes that people make when writing federal grant applications

❏ Discover the secrets of successful grantseekers

❏ Study a successful grant application

Identifying Types of Government Grants for Pre-K through 12 Schools

If you are searching for additional funding sources for students in grades pre-K through 12, government grant programs might be the way to go. There are many types of government grants available to the schools. They include city, county, state, and federal grants. You should be aware that city, county, and state grants may be "pass-through" grants for federal funds. That is, these agencies may receive monies outright from the federal government or receive funding after applying for a competitive grant. Once monies are received from the federal government, the cities, counties, or states then "pass" the funding onto the schools, usually through a competitive grant application process. Additional regulations and restrictions may be added to these pass-through grants, but no federal restrictions may be removed.

In addition to federal pass-through grants, a number of cities, counties, and states provide their own grant opportunities directly to schools. All government grant opportunities have a funding cycle, a specific application form, a set of criteria to evaluate proposals, and usually a staff and office to discuss programs and provide technical assistance.

The federal government continues to provide a source of external funding for pre-K–12 education. According to estimates from the U.S. Department of Education, $39.7 billion was spent on elementary and secondary education in FY 1999. This includes both *formula funding* and *discretionary funding* from the Department of Education, the Department of Health and Human Services, the Department of Agriculture, the Department of Energy, the Department of the Interior, and the Department of Defense. Although this figure seems high, it is only 9 percent of the total monies spent on education across the United States.[1]

Distinguishing between Formula Grants and Discretionary Grants

Formula grants (sometimes referred to as *direct grants*) are distributed to the schools through the various State Departments of Education or other *pass-through* agencies and are based upon data supplied by the applicant agency at the request of the funding agency. The funding agency, through a designated formula, then distributes the monies to eligible schools. For example, the Title 1, Part A Program (formerly Chapter 1) of the Elementary and Secondary Education Act might ask for the number of children in your school or school district on the free and reduced lunch program as a determinant of poverty in order to identify schools for this program. Other programs might ask for the number of non-English and limited English speaking students in your school or school district to determine needs in this area. By reporting back specific demographic data to the funding agency, districts and schools are funded based upon a predetermined formula. Normally, these types of grants do not require a competitive grant application process.

Discretionary grants are highly competitive and awarded on the basis of selection criteria developed by the funding agency. This type of grant is usually associated with a *Request for Proposal (RFP)* by the governmental agency. The government makes a reward of money or property in lieu of money (e.g., equipment) to a Local Education Agency (LEA) on the basis of how well it scored on the application's selection criteria. Those

[1]Digest of Education Statistics 1999, Chapter 4, Federal Programs for Education and Related Activities, Table 368, "Federal On-Budget Funds for Education." U.S. Department of Education, Washington, DC.

school districts fortunate to get funded usually receive a grant of one to three years, but are not guaranteed more than one year at a time.

Understanding Why Government Grants Are Difficult to Obtain

Competition for federal grant dollars is very keen, deadline dates can be very tight, and application requirements are extensive and cumbersome (25 to 100 pages). For example, in the 2000 funding cycle, only 14 percent of the *21st Century Community Learning Centers Program* applications were funded. Funding is usually made just once a year, so if you miss the funding deadline or find out about a program after the deadline date has passed, you have to wait until the following year to resubmit your application. While this is a disadvantage, you can actually turn it into an advantage for the following year. First, if your application was turned down, you will receive a copy of the scoring rubric from the funding agency with reviewer comments. (See scoring rubric for the "21st Century Community Learning Centers Program" in Appendix 2.) The comments will indicate where your strengths and weaknesses are. This is good to have as you plan for the next cycle of funding. Second, if you are turned down or missed the funding deadline, request copies of successful applications from school

"There goes Sally, delivering another one of those federal grant applications to the Post Office." (Cartoon by Dave Carpenter)

districts that have received grants. I have found that most school districts will cooperate with you on this. You might also want to check the websites of the funding agencies as many of them are now posting winning grants. Some books, such as this one, provide examples of winning grants. My philosophy has always been to keep a positive attitude, take advantage of what is offered to you, and if you are turned down or miss a deadline, apply next year or go to another funding agency with your ideas.

Many government grant opportunities are designed for schools and school districts with large numbers of minority students, large numbers of non-English and limited English speakers, serious academic and social needs, and located in poverty-stricken areas. If your school or school district fits any of these parameters, it is a perfect candidate for government funding. Otherwise, I would explore other funding opportunities discussed in this book including corporate and foundation grants and individual solicitation. That said, you should continue to keep an eye on federal and state grant opportunities that might fit your school's demographics and needs. Federal and state priorities change from time to time depending upon which political party is in office. What might not be considered important today may be considered vital tomorrow.

The following box shows a sampling of some of the federal government's discretionary grant programs for preschool through grade 12, including relevant web addresses. Familiarize yourself with these programs by going online to the agency's websites on a continuing basis. Because priorities change, it is important to check the websites often to stay updated and current on any new funding opportunities. The list presented is not exhaustive by any means and should be considered as a starting point for further prospect research. It is also recommended that you search the web site of your State Department of Education for specific opportunities in your state.

Sampling of Federal Government's Discretionary Grant Programs

U.S. Department of Education (http://www.ed.gov)

- Elementary School Counseling Demonstration Program
- Magnet Schools Assistance Programs
- Safe and Drug Free Schools
- Smaller Learning Communities Program
- Outreach Projects for Children with Disabilities
- Community Parent Resource Centers
- Public Charter Schools Program
- Bilingual Education: Comprehensive School/Program Development Grants
- Education Reform—Goals 2000
- Upward Bound Math/Science
- Technology Innovation Challenge Grant Program
- 21st Century Community Learning Centers
- Vocational and Adult Education Programs

U.S. Department of Health and Human Services (http://www.hhs.gov)

- Environmental Education Grants Program
- Headstart Programs

U.S. Department of Energy (http://www.doe.gov)

- Energy Conservation Program

National Science Foundation (http://www.nsf.org)

- Instructional Materials Development
- Informal Science Education
- Parent Involvement in Science, Mathematics, and Technology Education Initiative
- Teacher Enhancement
- Advanced Technological Education
- Urban Systemic Initiatives

National Endowment for the Humanities (http://www.neh.gov)

- Schools for a New Millennium
- National Education Projects
  —Materials Development
  —Curricular Development and Demonstration Projects

National Endowment for the Arts (http://www.nea.org)

- Education: Lifelong Education in the Arts (dance, visual arts, others)
  —Arts instruction
  —Artists in residence, workshops, or master classes
  —Performances, exhibitions, or demonstrations
  —Projects designed to provide positive alternatives for youth through the arts
  —Sequential lessons or courses in the arts
  —Research on the educational impact of the arts
  —Documentation and/or dissemination of promising programs and practices
  —Professional development for teachers, artists, and others working with students at the elementary or secondary school level

Improving Your Chances of Getting Funded

Teachers and administrators in the public schools have traditionally applied for federal grants through a process called *Request For Proposals (RFP)*. The most complete source for federal grant opportunities is the *Catalog of Federal Domestic Assistance (CFDA)* available on the World Wide Web at http://www.cfda.gov and published through the Superintendent of Documents, Washington, DC 20402. Each grant opportunity listed in the CFDA has a number assigned to it. *The Federal Register*, the government's daily newspaper, is available at www.acess.gpo.gov/sudocs/aces/aces140.html and through the Superintendent of Documents. It provides lists of legal rules and regulations and application deadlines for new grant programs.

Accessing the World Wide Web site of the U.S. Department of Education will keep you informed on new grant opportunities as they are announced. Its web address is www.ed.gov. Also access the website of your state Department of Education (SDOE) as well and your city and county governments for possible grant opportunities. There are links to all SDOE through the U.S. Department of Education website. City and county government websites can be obtained locally.

For busy teachers and administrators in the schools, there are a number of weekly publications that do the research for you and provide a summary of grant opportunities for pre-K–12 schools, including government, corporate, and foundation grants. You receive a newsletter each week that not only describes grant opportunities from the federal and state governments but also keeps you informed on corporate and foundation grants. Some of these publications are: *Education Grants Alert, Education Funding News, Grants to School Districts,* and *Federal Grants and Contracts Weekly.* Because subscriptions to these publications can be costly, you should contact your principal, district level coordinator, city or county librarian, or university librarian to find out if any of these publications are available to you. If not, you might want to have your school or school district purchase a subscription. It may well be worth the investment.

Many state Departments of Education are informed of federal grant opportunities and notify and alert school districts within their respective state. In some instances, the state Departments of Education conduct technical assistance meetings concerning federal grant opportunities for school districts within their states, and, in other instances, the federal agencies conduct their own technical assistance meetings. As federal funding diminishes, it is likely that we will see fewer technical assistance meetings conducted by the federal government.

Federal grant opportunities that originate in the U.S. Department of Education come under the Education Department's General Administrative Regulations (EDGAR). These regulations include instructions on grant application and selection criteria and assign a point total to each section

EDGAR Selection Criteria.

CRITERIA	MAXIMUM SCORE*
1. Meeting the purposes of authorizing statute	30
2. Extent of need for the project	20
3. Plan of operation	15
4. Quality of key personnel	7
5. Budget and cost effectiveness	5
6. Evaluation plan	5
7. Adequacy of resources	3
8. Weighting the criteria	15
TOTAL	100

*Can vary slightly based upon individual programs

of the proposal. Therefore, it is essential to be cognizant of the weight assigned to each section of the proposal to guide you in your proposal emphasis. Most federal grant opportunities follow the same selection criteria and point totals; however, you should check the point totals of the specific grant opportunity applied for. An example of the criteria and maximum score allowed taken from a federal grant application, Application For Federal Assistance, ED 424, is shown at the bottom of page 6. Note that the criteria and maximum score allowed sometimes change based upon the funding agency's criteria and emphasis.

Becoming Familiar with a Government Grant Application

The *Application for Federal Education Assistance (ED 424)* is a standard application format that is used by most funding agencies of the federal government. A shortened version of the application for the "21st Century Community Learning Centers" program appears in Appendix 1. To preserve space, the application does not include some of the introductory materials as well as some of the assurances pages that need to be signed off by the district's authorized representative (usually the superintendent).

Assignment 1

Applying for Government Grants

Using the Application For Federal Assistance (ED 424) in the Appendix, locate the Table of Contents and familiarize yourself with the overall contents of the application, including definitions, required forms, application checklist, and appendix. Carefully read the materials the Department of Education included as part of the application package, and be prepared to answer the following discussion questions:

1. What is the definition of a 21st Century Community Learning Centers Program?
2. What are the components of a high-quality after-school program?
3. Who is eligible to receive grants?
4. What will be the time period, size, and number of grants?
5. What kinds of program activities are required?
6. What absolute priority has the secretary added to the application process?
7. Name at least ten approved activities that can be used in the project.
8. What are the two competitive priorities that will apply to the competition?
9. What selection criteria will be used? Break out the point totals for each criterion.
10. What are the maximum number of pages that you can have for the program narrative?

Preparing a Government Grant Application for Funding

When preparing a government grant application for funding, it is critical that you follow the criteria very carefully and answer every question that the funding agency is concerned about. Be sure to present your data in the same sequence that the funding agency presents to you. This is very important because the people who read your grant proposal and score it do not want to spend a lot of time hunting for data. Your grant application should be well organized, clear, and concise. Anything you can do to help the reader find what he or she is looking for as quickly as possible will be much appreciated and scored accordingly. I actually repeat the *funding agency's own topic headings* in the narrative. Keep in mind that the people who are asked to read and score applications are usually assigned more applications than they would like and are looking for ways to separate the "good" from the "bad." You want your application to be exceptional, clear-cut, and stand out among the crowd. It is futile to have excellent ideas but be disorganized or miss a deadline.

Three Mistakes That Can Be Very Costly

I have found over the years that there are three common mistakes made over and over again by people applying for federal grants. These are:

1. Failing to read instructions carefully
2. Disregarding specific topic areas
3. Ignoring deadlines

Failing to Read Instructions Carefully

It is absolutely imperative that you read the instructions very carefully. The instructions set the parameters for your grant proposal and provide you with direction for completing each page of the application. Using the "21st Century Community Learning Centers Program Application" in Appendix 1 as an example, the instructions provide information concerning who is eligible to receive a grant; whether public and private agencies can participate; the time period, size, and number of grants that will be awarded; the regulations that apply to the program; the kinds of program activities that are required; priorities that apply to the grant competition; the selection criteria; and the point total that will be applied to each section. Instructions are also provided for completion of each page of the application such as the cover page, the program summary and abstract, the table of contents, the program narrative, the budget and budget narrative, assurances and required forms, and the appendix. Finally, an Application Checklist is provided that summarizes the complete application package. This is your last chance to make certain that you have followed all directions and that everything is included in your application package. If you are not thorough in reading the instructions carefully and providing the information requested, if your narrative exceeds the maximum number of pages allowed, if you single space instead of double space, or if you do not provide a table of contents, a program summary, a budget, and budget narrative, then you are not going to be very successful in obtaining grants.

Disregarding Specific Topic Areas

If you disregard specific topic areas that are required by the funding agency, you are asking for a denial of your funding request. For example, in the 21st Century Community Learning Centers Program Application for Grants, it states, "the Secretary will fund *only* those applications for 21st Century Community Learning Centers grants that include, among the array of services required and authorized by the statute, activities that offer significant expanded learning opportunities for children and youth in the community and that contribute to reduced drug use and violence." If your application for funding does not include this, you can be certain that you will not get funded. It is essential to address every specific topic area that the funding agency requires in your application for funding.

Ignoring Deadlines

If you ignore a deadline for any grant, you might as well kiss it good-bye. Though there are times when the government may extend a grant deadline for all applicants, a specific deadline is the most basic requirement you must fulfill. You can make certain to learn about extended deadlines by staying in close contact with your government representative or program officer and watch for announcements on the program website. Before you mail your grant application package, be sure to determine whether it must arrive in a specific office by a specific date and time or simply has to be postmarked by a specific date. These are two very different requirements. For example, if a grant application must arrive by a specific date and time, you should allow two extra days in transit to assure arrival by the deadline date. This is particularly critical for applicants in different parts of the country who will be sending grant application packages across several time zones. It would be a shame if you prepared a wonderful application but it arrived late. Be sure to send your application by overnight mail, courier, or other timely means. If using the U.S. Postal Service, always send it certified mail, return receipt requested, or some other means that requires a signature upon receipt. The overnight courier services will get a signature upon delivery. It is not an advantage to send your application off too early either, as most people feel that the application can be improved if they continue to refine and work on it up until the deadline time. A number of funding agencies merely require a postmark by a specific date to meet their deadline, rather than requiring that your application actually arrive by that date. Again, choose a secure mailing method with some type of signed return receipt.

Secrets of Successful Grantseekers

The successful grantseekers whom I have known have usually taken at least one course or workshop with a person who has been "on the firing line" and has had a great deal of experience and success with writing grants. People teaching these workshops and courses usually share their experiences, both good and bad, because regardless of how good you might be at writing grant proposals, you are probably not going to have every proposal accepted. Listed below are some of the secrets I have learned from successful grantseekers and from being on the firing line in the schools:

1. Do comprehensive prospect research on the Internet; in journals, newspapers, newsletters, and magazines; and through personal contacts to identify the funding opportunities in advance so that you have adequate time to prepare and complete your applications.

2. Have a very good idea of the basic rules of proposal writing and know how to work with stakeholders in large and small group settings to get the feedback and content needed to put the application together.

3. Have a comprehensive networking system in place that includes teachers, parents, community members, subject matter specialists, principals, grant writers, external evaluators, experts from colleges and universities, and others. All of these stakeholders can help in the formulation and writing of a successful grant application and can lend their names and expertise to the project.

4. Know that a superior application will state a project vision clearly and concisely, will document the needs convincingly, and will have overarching goals, measurable objectives, clearly stated activities, a realistic budget, and a comprehensive evaluation plan. Keep in mind also that the application needs to be creative, unique, convincing, and capture the imagination of the readers.

"Mom, how come Dad doesn't have to keep his room clean?"
(Cartoon by Dave Carpenter)

5. Know that the competition for obtaining grants is very keen, but you have the best chance for success if you prepare the proposal properly, follow the directions precisely, and respond to what the funding agency is looking for. It is also very important that the application be written with the EDGAR selection criteria in mind and that it be clearly and logically organized for the reader's ease.

Assignment 2

Preparing a Federal Grant Application for Funding

Having familiarized yourself with the most important parts of an Application for Federal Education Assistance (ED 424) for the 21st Century Community Learning Centers Program, you now have an opportunity to study an approved application for this same program, which appears in Chapter 7. Read the application carefully and be prepared to answer the following questions:

1. What needs assessment documentation is presented?
2. What is the overall goal of the program?
3. What are some of the objectives that the applicant presented?
4. Are you able to distinguish between the goal(s) and the objectives and why?
5. What activities or methods are presented to meet the objectives? Are these adequate and why?
6. What evaluation specifications are presented and are they measurable? Why?
7. Does the budget seem adequate to you? Why?

BIBLIOGRAPHY

1. **Education Funding News.** Education Funding Research Council, 4301 N. Fairfax Dr., Suite 875, Arlington, VA 22203. Lists corporate, foundation, and government grant opportunities for K-12 and offers suggestions on grant seeking. Published 50 times a year. Tel: (614) 382-3322

2. **Education Grants Alert.** Capitol Publications, 1101 King Street, Alexandria, VA 22314-2968. Lists corporate, foundation, and government oppportunities for K-12 and offers suggestions for grant seeking. Published 50 times per year. Tel: (800) 655-5597

3. **Grants to School Districts.** Quinlan Publishing Company, 23 Drydock Ave., Boston, MA 02210-9877. Lists corporate, foundation, and government grant opportunities for K-12. Published 50 times per year. Tel: (617) 542 0048

4. **Federal Grants and Contracts Weekly.** Capitol Publications, 1101 King Street, Alexandria, VA 22314-2968. Lists grant and contract opportunities from the federal government and tips on how to prepare proposals. Published 50 times a year. Tel: (800) 655-5597

5. **Research Grant Guides, Inc.** 12798 W. Forest Hill Blvd., Suite 304, West Palm Beach, FL 33414-4704. Publishes directories of operating grants, equipment grants, program grants, computer and high technology grants, and others. Tel: (561) 795-6129

2
Applying for Corporate and Foundation Grants

In this chapter you will

❐ Identify the many types of corporate and foundation grant opportunities available to the schools

❐ Understand why corporate and foundation grants might be easier to get than government grants

❐ Discover a step-by-step strategy for winning corporate and foundation funding for the public schools including prospect research

❐ Identify some corporations and foundations interested in giving grants and gifts to the public schools

Corporate and Foundation Grant Opportunities

One of the great resources for corporate and foundation funding and information is the *Foundation Center* in New York City. Established by several foundations in 1956, the Foundation Center's mission is to foster public awareness and understanding of the foundation field. The Foundation Center reports that there are more than 51,000 corporate, independent, and community foundations in the United States, with the number growing weekly. The total assets of these foundations are more than $385 billion. They estimate that this group contributed more than $22.8 billion to worthy causes in 1999 alone with vigorous growth expected well into the future. Sara Engelhardt, President of the Foundation Center, stated in a recent press release, "Foundation giving continues to expand, affording new possibilities for ameliorating social ills, enriching lives in our communities, improving the chances for all children, and increasing knowledge in all fields of endeavor. This trend is fueled by many factors—new donors and new foundations, a strong economy, and a healthy corporate sector. This means that we can probably count on vigorous growth in foundation giving well into the future."[1]

Foundations are required by federal tax law to give away an average of at least *5 percent* of their assets to charity over a three-year period. As foundation assets and businesses continue to grow and as individuals and families begin to inherit enormous amounts of wealth and establish their own foundations, the opportunities look bright for the public schools to tap into this vast market. Why not? Private schools, colleges, universities, and nonprofit organizations have been reaping the rewards for years!

Corporate Giving

Corporations provide support to nonprofit organizations, including the schools, through their own private foundations, direct-giving programs, or both. Corporate foundations, with total assets of more than $13 billion, give more than $2.4 billion to worthy causes each year. These separate legal entities maintain close ties with their parent organizations and their giving philosophies usually mirror company priorities and interests. Corporate foundations are required to follow the laws and regulations governing private foundations, including filing an annual Form 990-PF with the Internal Revenue Service. The 990-PF provides a complete grants list, the names of the foundation's trustees and officers, and other relevant information. Having access to 990-PFs will assist you in determining the giving trends of a particular foundation as well as the size of the grants made and other vital data. Fortunately, 990-PFs are public records and you can access these documents through the GrantsSmart link at *http://www.Grant Smart.org* and other search engines including the cooperating libraries of the Foundation Center and tax returns for foundations in state attorneys general offices. For additional information on accessing 990-PF Forms, go to *http://www.fdncenter.org/onlib/faqs/990pf.html.*

In addition to corporate foundations, corporations are also involved in *direct-giving programs*. These giving programs are not separately incorporated and the IRS does not require the corporation to adhere to private foundation laws or regulations, including the filing of Form 990-PF. Corporations are allowed to deduct up to 10 percent of their pre-tax income for charitable purposes.

Over the years, I have discovered that corporations are interested in forming partnerships with the public schools and in contributing dollars and equipment to them. They are also involved in providing technical assistance, including in-kind assistance such as staffing for particular projects like wiring schools for the Internet or providing speakers for classes and career days. It is important to understand that corporations typically contribute in those communities where their employees live and work; therefore, it is not recommended that you apply for these grants out of your area.

---

[1]Press Release dated March 29, 2000, The Foundation Center, New York.

Independent Foundations

Independent (private) foundations, with total assets over $326 billion, contributed more than $14 billion to worthy causes in 1998. These foundations are nongovernmental, usually have a principal fund or endowment, are managed by a board of trustees and directors, and give cash and gifts to nonprofit organizations, including the schools. America's 1,000 leading private foundations have given more than $5 billion annually to colleges, universities, nonprofit organizations, and the schools. They typically support charitable, educational, religious, and other causes that serve the public good.

Over the years, I have discovered that independent foundations are interested in funding "excellence" in the public schools. They typically have not been interested in compensatory education or remedial types of programs, although some foundations do support these efforts. Independent foundations are concerned with bringing about change in a positive manner or in enhancing and supplementing existing programs. Some foundations support math, science, and the environment while others are interested in music, art, and dance. Other foundations give preference to computer technology and literacy, while still others are interested in health education, parent education, and staff development. Some independent foundations support capital equipment such as computers, printers, scanners, video, and sound—however, only insofar as the equipment is directly related to a clear vision and an overall program plan. In other words, they normally do not fund hardware only.

Community Foundations

There are more than 400 community foundations across the United States with total assets of more than $30 billion. These foundations gave away more than $1.9 billion in 1999 to good causes. Community foundations are financially supported by individuals, businesses, and organizations in a specific community or region. Within certain parameters, anyone can be a donor to a community foundation. Donors can give assets of cash, stock, bonds, real estate, and others. These gifts can usually be made within the lifetime of the donors or through their estates, with the donors receiving maximum tax benefits.

There are community foundations located in every state in the United States. Grants from these foundations help to support charitable groups and programs working to improve the quality of life within a specific community or region. Over the past several years, I have observed community foundations become more interested in the public schools. Competitive grant programs such as teachers' funds to assist classroom teachers with mini-grants for innovative programs have been established. Other types of innovative grants are also being made to schools to provide funding for programs that improve teaching and learning in the classroom. Community foundations are sprouting up all over the country. They are a good source of funding for teachers, schools, and school districts. Take the time to locate the community foundations in your area of the country.

Obtaining Corporate and Foundation Funding Is Easier Than You Think

There are three good reasons for applying for corporate and foundation funding at this time. They are:

1. **Corporations and foundations are interested in providing grants to schools, and many teachers and administrators have not yet discovered this funding opportunity.** Are we sneaky or what? If you know how to obtain corporate and foundation funding, you will be at an advantage over other people who are not yet aware of this funding source. Therefore, by having fewer people apply for corporate and foundation grants, competition will not be as keen as for applying for grant opportunities that are more well known such as federal grants. This, of course, will not be going on forever, so take advantage of it now and reap the rewards. A word of caution should be mentioned. Just because a corporation or foundation indicates in its literature that it funds education doesn't necessarily mean that it funds K-12 education. Make sure that you read the eligibility guidelines very carefully to determine this before you apply for funding.

2. **Most corporate and foundation funding agencies require an application of just two to ten pages or a one-page letter of application.** Is this good, or what? This is reason enough to apply for corporate and foundation funding. Teachers and administrators are very busy people. So are program officers and other staff at the funding agencies. By keeping application requirements short and to the point, everybody wins.

3. **Most corporations and foundations fund more than once a year.** This is a delight! Some of these agencies fund four times a year, and others fund every time the board meets, which could be twelve times a year. The funding timetables are much more favorable than government funding timetables of once a year. If you a miss a federal government grant deadline or get turned down, you are out of luck for an entire year. If you miss a corporate or foundation deadline, you have an opportunity to apply in another month or two or go to another funding agency with your project.

While I do not want to leave you with the impression that it is easy to obtain monies from corporations and foundations, I do want to point out that in my experience working in the public schools, I found that obtaining corporate and foundation funding was less demanding than obtaining government grants. I have also discovered that obtaining these grants takes more nurturing and personal contact. Some people like this, and others do not. Corporations and foundations want to feel that their money will be well spent if they award you a grant. Many of these funding agencies are becoming more and more interested in the evaluation component of your grant application and the evaluation results. They want to be able to report to their board about the positive impact their funding has had on the schools. They desire to get to know you and want to feel confident in your proposed project and your school district's ability to "deliver."

A Step-by-Step Strategy for Winning Corporate and Foundation Funding for Pre-K through 12 Schools

Below is a step-by-step strategy for winning corporate and foundation funding for pre-K through 12 schools. It has proven successful in my work in the schools and should be helpful and practical to you as you endeavor to obtain funding from corporations and foundations.

STEP 1.   Have an innovative idea and vision in mind. Generate your ideas from teams of two to five people. These teams should be made up of people having similar ideas and visions for funding. Obtain administrative support for your idea. Ask for release time to write your project if funds are available for this purpose.

STEP 2.   Begin to do *prospect research* by becoming familiar with corporate and foundation funding agencies in your local area, the state, and the nation that are interested in funding pre-K–12 education programs. It is usually easier to obtain monies from local and statewide foundations and corporations rather than national foundations that traditionally fund projects having national implications and significance. However, if your project meets the criteria of any of the national foundations, go for it.

STEP 3.   Access the Foundation Center website at *http://fdncenter.org* to locate corporations and foundations in your area, including community foundations that might be interested in making grants to the schools. The Foundation Center website, which is free, is loaded with worthwhile information for people doing basic research on corporate and foundation giving. For a fee, people seeking more in-depth coverage can purchase the Foundation Center's Database on CD-ROM (FC Search 4.0), which features a comprehensive listing of active U.S. foundations and corporate giving programs and their associated grants. It includes a *Grantmaker File* of more than 53,000 records and a *Grants File* with more than 210,000 grants of $10,000 or more awarded by the nation's largest funders. This database is also available for free through the Foundation Center's main cooperating collections located in New York City, Washington, DC, Atlanta, Cleveland, and San Francisco, and in smaller cooperating collections located all across the United States. You can find out where these locations are by accessing *http://fdncenter.org/collections/index.html*. In addition to programs such as FC Search 4.0, there are other materials that you can use to do prospect research. Some are hard copy, more traditional types of books and others are on

CD-ROM (see Bibliography). In addition to studying the materials and locating foundations and corporations having the same interests as yours, also access the links leading to the 990-PF Forms to discover the giving patterns and trends of corporations and foundations in your area. Visit the fundraising resource libraries in your school, district office, county office, and the colleges and universities in your area. Before you know it, you are going to have many funding resources available to you.

STEP 4.   Once you have completed the prospect research phase, you are now ready to request the most recent information, yearbooks, and applications from the corporations and foundations that are potential funding sources for your school or district. This can usually be accomplished via e-mail, by telephone or fax, or by writing directly to the corporation or foundation. In school districts or counties where corporate and foundation files are kept up to date, contact the district or county person who is responsible for fundraising and ask for assistance, or go onto the district website to look for grants and grant writing links if the district has moved in this direction. See an example at *http://www.sowashco.k12.mn.us/grants/linkspage.htm.*

STEP 5.   Make multiple copies of relevant applications and materials and read and study carefully. Reread several times. Check to see if there are any deadline dates of which you need to be aware. Discover how many public school projects were funded previously, including the amounts of funding. Pinpoint the deadline dates on your calendar.

STEP 6.   If possible, telephone the program officer at the foundation or corporation to discuss your ideas and to begin the "nurturing process." Make certain that you are thoroughly familiar with your project and that you are able to discuss it with clarity, conviction, and strength. Also, be prepared to respond to any questions or concerns of the program officer and incorporate any relevant suggestions for improvement. For example, one question that is often asked is "How are you planning to evaluate this project?" If it appears that the program officer is interested in your project and that monies are available to meet your needs based upon your prospect research, ask for an appointment to visit the foundation with your site or district level administrator. In instances where you are requesting a considerable amount of money, it is recommended that you invite your superintendent of schools and a board member to join you in meeting with the chief operating officer of the foundation. This person-to-person contact, especially with the heads of both organizations, could do wonders for your corporate and foundation fundraising effort. In fact, this approach is used on a continuing basis by private schools, colleges, universities, and nonprofit organizations. College and university presidents are "on the road" on a continuing basis soliciting funds. Why can't superintendents of schools make this part of their job description? Recently, a superintendent and I visited two major foundations in San Francisco. In each instance, the chief operating officer of the foundation commented, "This is the first time that I have ever met with a superintendent of schools in my office." I turned to the superintendent and asked, "Are we on the right track?" Needless to say, we were funded by both foundations.

STEP 7. If you are unable to visit the funding agency, invite the program officer of the funding agency and other staff members to visit you. If there appears to be no interest in any visitations or in having you submit an application, go on to another funding agency with your ideas.

STEP 8. If you are fortunate enough to have the funding agency indicate that it would like to make a site visit, then you are on the right track for getting funded. This is one of the key indicators that the funding agency is interested in your project. Sometimes a site visit might not be scheduled until after you submit an application. In either case, you have good reason to get a little excited. Determine how much time the program officer will spend in the district, including arrival and departure times. Prepare carefully for the visitation. Include an agenda that will be mailed out to the visitor and other invited guests ahead of time. Invite key people to the entrance and exit meetings, including the superintendent, principal(s), one or two board members, and representative parents and teachers. Meet the program officer at the airport, if this person is arriving by plane. Provide for food, snacks, lunch, and lodging, if appropriate. Your goal is to impress the visitor with your school or school district and proposed project. Upon arrival at the *entrance meeting*, which could take place at the district office or at a school site, introduce the program officer and other visitors, if appropriate, to each person at the meeting, and then proceed to review the day's activities with everyone. Follow your time schedule and agenda very carefully, leaving time for classroom visitations and observations (if appropriate), lunch, followup, and the scheduled *exit meeting*. The same people who were invited to the entrance meeting should be invited to the exit meeting. The goal of the exit meeting is to ascertain whether the program officer is impressed with what was seen and whether the program officer is ready to recommend the district for funding. In a number of instances, I have witnessed program officers at exit meetings tell district officials that they were so impressed with what they had seen that they were prepared to recommend the district for funding. They went on further to request that the district put together an application of three to five pages asking for x number of dollars. In instances when the program officer does not disclose this information to the group, I believe it would be appropriate to ask the following questions: "What impressed you the most about your visit today?" "Do you have any suggestions for improvement?" "Are you planning to recommend us for funding?" "How much funding should we be requesting?" **Note:** Have a carefully prepared budget available that is categorized and well thought out (see pages 63–66). Also indicate how much the district is going to contribute to the project. You can use "in-kind" contributions for this purpose, such as staff assigned to coordinate and facilitate the project, facilities that you will be using, utility and custodial costs, and costs for materials and equipment.

"This is all part of the corporate and foundation nurturing process I've been telling you about." (Cartoon by Dave Carpenter)

STEP 9.   Whether you have arranged for a site visit or have been encouraged to submit an application without a site visit, begin to fill in the application, responding specifically to what the funding agency is asking. **Note:** In some instances, the corporate or independent foundation does not provide an application. It merely will tell you to respond to its guidelines. If this is the case, it is recommended that you use a *prototype application*, making sure that you cover the needs, goals, objectives, activities, evaluation specifications, and budget. Some states have a *common application form* that is recognized by most foundations in the state. If this is the case, ask where you can obtain a copy of the application and study it carefully. Also, note that some corporations and foundations will ask for just a one- to two-page letter of request. This you will appreciate very much. Always give the funding agency exactly what they ask for, nothing more, nothing less. After you have responded to the funding agency's guidelines and have completed a first draft of the application or letter, go over it carefully to correct spelling, typographical errors, grammar, and word usage.

STEP 10. Have one or two persons who are not in your field of interest read the completed application for clarity and input. Also, have one or two persons in your field of interest read it as well. Ask for assistance when formulating your budget, including proper budget categorizing and cost breakdowns. In many school districts, the person to go to for help would be the business manager, district accountant, or site principal. It is essential to present to the funding agency a realistic, concise budget, providing explanations where appropriate.

STEP 11. After you have completed step 10 above, put together your final draft, including a cover letter that "grabs" the reader. The cover letter is usually one page and provides a brief summary of the project with all the necessary details (see page 150 for sample cover letter). Obtain needed signatures and approvals, do necessary proofreading, and make final corrections. Mail your application to the funding agency "return receipt requested" or forward by another means in plenty of time to meet the funding deadline. Some funding agencies are now accepting proposals electronically, and others are providing applications online. Make certain that you are using the correct format for each funding agency to which you apply.

Requests for Proposals (RFPs)

Some corporations and foundations announce *Requests for Proposals (RFPs)* on their websites, in newsletters, and in publications like *Education Funding News*, *Education Grants Alert*, and *Grants to School Districts*. By announcing an RFP, the funding agency is *pinpointing* and *targeting* its monies in specific interest areas. To some agencies, this is positive in that they will receive applications that respond to a specific need or concern of the agency. As a school or a school district, there are advantages and disadvantages in responding to an RFP. The first advantage is that you already know what the foundation is interested in by the materials that it provides in the RFP package. Second, you will probably be told for what size grant to apply and how many grants will get funded. One of the major disadvantages of responding to an RFP is that your focus will be narrowed down to the specific interest area of the funding agency. Of course, if your interests match the funding agency's interest area, this is not a problem. Another disadvantage would be that you will probably have more competition in obtaining the grant if the foundation announces it to the world via its website and through other publications. More people generally respond to an RFP than do people making individual contacts with foundations. I would recommended that if you do respond to an RFP, use the same techniques recommended in this text.

Some Corporations and Foundations Interested in Giving Grants and Gifts to the Public Schools

Most grantseekers today are involved in accessing the World Wide Web to obtain needed information and applications. I have identified a list of potential corporate and foundation funding resources and their web addresses. These agencies have expressed an interest in funding pre-K through 12th grade programs; however, because funding priorities and interests change from time to time, it is very important to keep up to date and confirm with the agency what its interests are at the time of your investigation. It is possible that some of the agencies identified here have changed their funding priorities. For this reason, make certain that your prospect research is current. The list provided is not exhaustive by any means. It is rather a starting point to head you in the right direction of potential funding sources. By accessing the websites below, including other websites, links, and resources listed elsewhere in this book, you will become familiar with the vast array of funding opportunities available to you.

Funding Agency	Web Address (all begin with http://)
Abbott Laboratories	www.abbott.com/community
AT&T Foundation	www.att.com/foundation/
BankAmerica Corporation	www.bankamerica.com/community
Bill & Melinda Gates Foundation	www.gatesfoundation.org
Chevron Corporation	www.chevron.com/community
Coca-Cola Foundation	www.coca-colacompany.com/foundation/index.html
Crail-Johnson Foundation	www.crail-johnson.org/
Cisco Systems Foundation	www.cisco.com/edu
Deere & Company	www.deere.com/
DeWitt Wallace-Reader's Digest Fund	www.wallacefunds.org
Dow Chemical	www.dow.com/about/corp/social/gen-fund.htm
Hewlett-Packard Company	www.webcenter.hp.com/grants/
International Business Machines	www.ibm.com/IBM/IBMGives
James S. and James L. Knight Foundation	www.knightfdn.org

Funding Agency	*Web Address (all begin with http://)*
MacDonald's Corporation	www.rmhc.com/grant/index.html
Medtronic Foundation	www.medtronic.com/foundation
Metropolitan Life Insurance Co.	www.metlife.com/Companyinfo/ Community/Found/Index.html
Microsoft Corporation	www.microsoft.com/giving
NEC Foundation of America	www.nec.com/company/ foundation
J.C. Penney Company	www.jcpenney.net/company/ commrel/index.htm
Prudential Insurance Co.	www.prudential.com/community/
Sara Lee Corporation	www.saraleefoundation.org
Sprint Corporation	www.sprint.com/sprint/overview/ commun.html
Stuart Foundation	www.stuartfoundation.org
Toyota Motor Sales	www.nsta.org/programs/tapestry
Verizon Foundation	www.verizon.com/foundation
William and Flora Hewlett Foundation	www.hewlett.org
Weyerhaeuser Company	www.weyerhaeuser.com/ citizenship/default.asp
W.M. Keck Foundation	www.wmkeck.org/

Assignment

Corporate And Foundation Grants

1. Identify an area of need and interest for which you would like to seek funding.
2. Do prospect research on the World Wide Web or through publications and materials listed below to match up your needs with at least two funding agencies' interests.
3. Once you have at least two possible match-ups, download as much information from each funding agency's website, including applications, recent grants made, and other vital information. If information cannot be accessed and downloaded, request information from the funding agency by phone or through the mail.
4. Access the 990PF forms for each identified foundation and study funding trends and grant amounts awarded.
5. After reviewing the information very carefully, be prepared to meet in groups of three to five to discuss and share the following:
   a. What area(s) have the funding agencies indentified as their areas of interest at this time? Do these areas of interest match yours?
   b. What kind of application do these funding agencies require? Provide copies of the application to each member of the group.
   c. When are the application deadlines?
   d. Are there any funding restrictions concerning geographical areas?
   e. Have the identified funding agencies made grants previously to the public schools? What was the average size of the grants?
   f. What do you believe are your chances of getting funded from each of the funding agencies? Why?

BIBLIOGRAPHY

Software

1. **FC Search: The Foundation Center's Database on CD-ROM.** Foundation Center, 75 Fifth Avenue, New York, NY 10003-3076. Includes more than 40,000 U.S. foundations and corporate givers in a fully searchable CD-ROM format. Tel. (800) 424-9836

2. **The Grants Database on CD-ROM.** Oryx Press, P.O. Box 33889, Phoenix, AZ 85067-3889. Lists corporate, foundation and government grant opportunities on CD-ROM, including deadlines for funding. Updated every other month. Tel. (602) 265-6250

3. **Grants on Disk.** The Taft Group, 835 Penobscot Building, 645 Griswold Street, Detroit, MI. 48226-4094. CD-ROM lists wide variety of corporate and foundation grants recently awarded and provides profiles of the grant makers. Includes quarterly updates. Tel. (800) 877-8238

4. **GrantScape: CFDA.** Capitol Publications, P.O. Box 1453, Alexandria, VA 22313-2053. Comprehensive listing of federal funds available and how to apply to the funding agencies. Includes program objectives, agency authorization and types of assistance available. Tel. (800) 655-5597

5. **Prospector's Choice.** The Taft Group, 835 Penobscot Building, 645 Griswold Street, Detroit, MI. 48226-4094. CD-ROM profiles more than 10,000 foundations and corporate giving programs, including biographical information on the officers and directors and samples of grants each organization made. Updated annually. Tel. (800) 877-8238

Directories and Guides

1. **Directory of Computer and High Technology Grants, Third Edition.** Richard M. Eckstein, Editor, Research Grant Guides, Inc. P.O. Box 1214, Loxahatchee, FL 33470. Profiles 500 foundations that award technology grants to schools and nonprofits. Lists Internet resources. Revisions made on a continuing basis. Tel: (561) 795-6129

2. **Directory of Corporate and Foundation Givers**. The TAFT Group, 835 Penobscot Building, 645 Griswold Street, Detroit, MI 48226-4094 (two volumes). A national listing of more than 8,000 major funding sources for nonprofits. Revisions made on a continuing basis. Tel: (800) 877-8238

3. **Funding Sources for K-12 Schools and Adult Basic Education.** Oryx Press, P.O. Box 33889, Phoenix, AZ 85067-3889. Profiles more than 1,000 foundations, corporate-giving programs, federal agencies, and others who give to elementary, secondary, and adult basic education programs. Tel: (602) 265-6250

4. **Grants for Elementary and Secondary Education.** The Foundation Center, 75 Fifth Avenue, New York, NY 10003-3076. Lists grants of $10,000 or more for elementary and secondary education. Revisions made on a continuing basis. Tel: (800) 424-9836

5. **Grants for School Technology.** Capitol Publications, 1101 King Street, Suite 444, Alexandria, VA 22314-2968. Profiles more than 200 corporations and foundations that make grants to elementary and secondary education. Revisions made on a continuing basis. Tel: (800) 655-5597

6. **Grants for Science and Technology Programs.** The Foundation Center, 75 Fifth Avenue, New York, NY 10003-3076. Lists grants of $10,000 or more for science and technology programs. Revisions made on a continuing basis. Tel: (800) 424-9836

7. **National Guide to Funding for Children, Youth, and Families.** The Foundation Center, 75 Fifth Avenue, New York, NY 10003-3076. Profiles more than 3,000 foundations and corporations that give to children, youth, and families. Lists over 13,000 recently awarded grants. Revisions made on a continuing basis. Tel: (800) 424-9836

8. **National Guide to Funding for Elementary and Secondary Education.** The Foundation Center, 75 Fifth Avenue, New York, NY 10003-3076. Profiles more than 3,000 corporate and foundation giving programs that serve children, youth, and families. Revisions made on a continuing basis. Tel: (212) 620-4230

9. **The School Technology Funding Directory, 2001 Edition.** 7920 Norfolk Ave., Suite 900, Bethesda, MD 20814. Desktop reference to $30 billion in school technology funding. Includes more than 500 grants and funding sources in the K-12 technology market. Tel: (800) 394-0115

Periodicals

1. *Chronicle of Philanthropy.* The Chronicle of Philanthropy, P.O. Box 1989, Marion, OH 43305-1989. Newspaper of the nonprofit world published 24 times a year. Provides news and information for grant seekers, including lists of grants, fundraising ideas and techniques, statistics, updates on regulations, forthcoming conferences, and other relevant information. Also publishes on a yearly basis *The Nonprofit Handbook*, with listing of books, periodicals, software, Internet sites, and other essential resources for nonprofit leaders. Tel: (614) 382-3322

2. *Education Funding News.* Education Funding Research Council, 4301 N. Fairfax Dr., Suite 875, Arlington, VA 22203. Lists corporate, foundation, and government grant opportunities for K-12 and offers suggestions on grant seeking. Published 50 times a year. Tel: (703) 528-1000

3. *Education Grants Alert.* Capitol Publications, 1101 King Street, Alexandria, VA 22314-2968. Lists corporate, foundation, and government grant opportunities for K-12 and offers suggestions on grant seeking. Published 50 times a year. Tel: (800) 655-5597

4. *Foundation and Corporate Grants Alert.* Capitol Publications, 1101 King Street, Alexandria, VA 22314-2968. Published monthly. Lists grant opportunities, profiles foundations and corporate-giving programs and grant priorities, and provides helpful suggestions. Tel: (800) 655-5597

5. *Foundation News and Commentary.* Council on Foundations, 1828 L Street, NW, 3rd Floor, Washington, DC 20036. Provides articles, case studies, questions and answers, and essays on critical issues confronting philanthropy today. News and information on emerging technologies, ethics, regulations, legislation, research, book reviews, and grantmaking videos. Tel: (800) 771-8187

6. *School Technology Funding Bulletin.* 7920 Norfolk Ave., Suite 900, Bethesda, MD 20814. News, tools, and grants listings to help capture some of the $30 billion in school technology funding. Funding success stories, grant analysis, latest listings of new and hidden grant opportunities, techniques, and unwritten rules from some of the nation's successful grant writing consultants. Tel: (800) 394-0115

Web Reports and Websites

1. Foundation Center Website. The most comprehensive website for corporate and foundation grant seeking. Has links to hundreds of funders and other relevant sites.
    http://www.fdncenter.org

2. 50 Largest Corporate Foundations by Total Giving.
    http://fdncenter.org/grantmaker/trends/top50giving.html

3. Top 100 U.S. Foundations by Total Giving.
    http://fdncenter.org/grantmaker/trends/top100giving.html

4. 25 Largest Community Foundations by Total Giving.
    http://fdncenter.org/grantmaker/trends/top25giving.html

5. eSchool News Website. A good news source for K–12 technology, including funding opportunities, publications, announcements, conferences, and related links.
    http://www.eschoolnews.org

6. Public Education Network Website. Provides information on how to start a Local Education Foundation including characteristics, mission, bylaws, committees, meetings, staff, office, and twenty-one steps to follow when forming a LEF. Also includes a free weekly newspaper.
    http://www.publiceducation.org

3

Individual Solicitation and the Public Schools

In this chapter you will

- ❐ Learn the significance and impact of individual giving in the private and public sectors of the United States
- ❐ Identify some major gifts given to the public schools
- ❐ Learn how to "gear up" for a program of individual solicitation that includes forming a school or district foundation
- ❐ Identify methods to organize your fundraising effort
- ❐ Distinguish between an "annual campaign" and a "capital campaign"
- ❐ Learn a six-step approach to individual solicitation
- ❐ Become familiar with what a "pledge card" looks like
- ❐ Learn about "planned giving"
- ❐ Identify possible gift ideas for the public schools

Significance and Impact of Individual Giving

Individual solicitation of gifts from wealthy individuals and others is practically nonexistent in the public schools. There are many reasons for this, but suffice it to say that teachers and administrators have been reluctant as a group to ask constituents for major gifts of cash, materials, equipment, and buildings. Maybe it is because the public schools are tax supported that inhibits them from asking. However, so are the University of California, the State University of New York, the University of Michigan, the University of Iowa, and other state-supported institutions. These entities have been raising billions of dollars each year while the public schools have been idly standing by. I believe the major reason the public schools have not been soliciting major gifts from potential donors is because superintendents of schools, principals, classroom teachers, board members, and parents are inexperienced in asking for major gifts and have been reluctant to ask. This must change if the public schools are to compete for needed dollars.

According to an article in the July 24, 2000 edition of *Time* magazine called "The New Philanthropists," the United States has produced more millionaires and billionaires than any other nation. It was stated that 73 percent of Americans reported giving money to charity in 1999. Paul Schervisch and John Havens, authors of a Boston College study on giving, estimate that $41 trillion will be left by aging baby boomers to their heirs and charities in the coming years. The American Association of Fundraising Council (AAFRC) Trust For Philanthropy stated in its report, *Giving USA 2000*, that when the twentieth century ended, charitable giving surpassed $190 billion. They indicated that contributions from individuals showed the greatest gain reaching approximately $143.71 billion in 1999, with bequests totaling $15.61 billion. These two figures added together are responsible for more than 82 percent of all contributions coming from individuals. This is shown in Figure 3.1. In breaking out the contributions by recipient type, *Giving USA 2000* showed that education was the second highest recipient, after religion, totaling $27.46 billion (see Figure 3.2).

FIGURE 3.1   1999 Contributions: $190.16 billion by source of contribution.

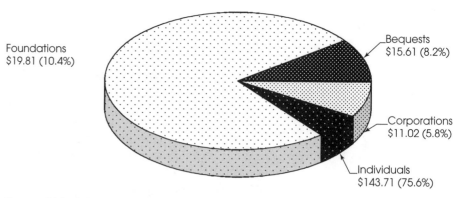

Foundations
$19.81 (10.4%)

Bequests
$15.61 (8.2%)

Corporations
$11.02 (5.8%)

Individuals
$143.71 (75.6%)

Source: Giving USA 2000/AAFRC Trust for Philanthropy.

FIGURE 3.2   1999 Contributions: $190.16 billion type of recipient organization.

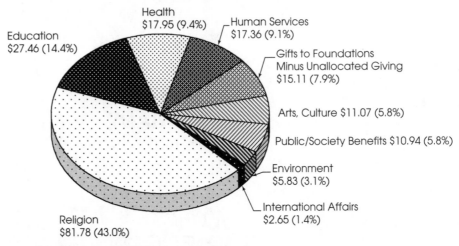

Source: Giving USA 2000/AAFRC Trust for Philanthropy.

Getting Ready for the Big Boom in Philanthropy

In addition to the statistics and optimistic projections presented, the high-tech phenomenon has made more people richer faster than in any time in our history. What does all this mean? It means that the public schools are at the threshold of one of the biggest booms in the history of philanthropy, and we need to "crank up" our systems. School districts must begin to employ full-time development staff and consultants to assist the schools in learning how to ask for and obtain major grants and gifts. With realistic expectations, the new staff become a "profit center" for the school district. Superintendents and principals must begin to think like presidents of universities when it comes to fundraising and get out and meet some of their wealthy constituents and invite them into their homes.

The most successful CEOs are on the road 25 percent of the time meeting and nurturing potential funding sources. Superintendents of schools need to be doing the same. School board members, because of their contacts in the community, should become part of the overall fundraising effort and participate in a training program as needed.

Every day of every year people are giving to good causes. Public education is obviously a good cause. The schools have such great potential for raising serious money. All they have to do is find out how and ask! Instead of concentrating on bake sales, car washes, pizza sales, gift wrap sales, and other "nickel and dime" fundraising efforts, people affiliated with the public schools should be exploring ways to bring in major dollars that will have a positive impact on children, programs, and schools. They understand that most of our business, scientific, political, and educational leaders are products of the public schools, and they want to see the schools succeed.

(Cartoon by Dave Carpenter)

What Needs Do Public Schools Have?

There is a need across the United States for increased funding for the public schools. Our tax base, just like the tax base for the state-supported colleges and universities, is not enough to provide a "world-class" education for all our children. The schools need additional funding for new and innovative program offerings, including programs in the arts, mathematics, sciences, English language development, and foreign languages. Monies are needed for new technology, including computers, printers, scanners, and software. Teachers need additional staff development to help keep them up to date with changing curricula and changing technology. Budgets are already strained paying for competitive teacher salaries and fringe benefits, maintaining buildings and grounds, acquiring land, building new facilities, and remodeling existing ones. Because these urgent needs are beginning to become known around the nation, we are starting to see money and other gifts flow to the public schools like never before.

Until recently, most of the charitable giving for education has gone to the colleges, universities, private schools, and nonprofit organizations. These entities, for the most part, are well organized, knowledgeable, and well trained. The public schools are in their infancy when it comes to fundraising on a grand scale. There is no agency at this time that gathers statistical data on charitable giving to the public schools. We do know, however, that a number of major grants and gifts to the schools have been received in recent years. The following box lists some examples of these gifts.

Examples of Major Gifts Given to the Public Schools*

- Former Ambassador Walter Annenberg's $500 million gift, called the Annenberg Challenge, to bring about systemic change in large urban school systems, rural school systems, and arts education in major cities.
- The Bill and Melinda Gates Foundation's $350 million gift aimed at improving our nation's schools, including a $56 million gift to support the design and development of small schools.
- The Wallace-Readers Digest Funds have pledged $150 million over five years to a new grants program to improve the leadership of public schools and school districts. The money will be focused on efforts to recruit, train, and retain high-quality principals and superintendents.
- Former Netscape CEO, Jim Barksdale, and his wife Sally, created a $100 million endowment to advance literacy in the schools in their home state of Mississippi.
- Retired Wal-Mart Corporation president, Ferold Arend, and his wife Jane, gave a gift of $5 million to build an art center at Bentonville High School in Arkansas, and an associate Wal-Mart executive, Jack Shewmaker, and his family, added an additional $1 million to equip the center.
- A 1947 alumnus of Escondido High School in California, Bob Wilson, and his wife Marion, gave a $1 million donation to renovate the school's football stadium.
- Ed Cherry, a retired physical education teacher in La Mesa Spring Valley School District in California, set up a scholarship fund for students at the Parkway Middle School to encourage them to go on to college.

*These are some examples of grants and gifts that have been made. This is by no means a complete list.

(continued)

- Philanthropists with the New Schools Venture Fund in the Silicon Valley, headed by John Doerr of Kleiner Perkins, have set aside $20 million for educational entrepreneurs and educational start-up companies.
- Hundreds of taxpayers in Philadelphia and other parts of Pennsylvania, encouraged by newspaper editorials, donated their $100 state tax rebate checks to the public schools of their choice in November 2000.
- The Open Society Institute in New York City awarded a grant of $229,000 to the Baltimore Public Schools to develop a plan to improve academic performance in zoned high schools in Baltimore City Public School System.

"I realize that a 5 million dollar contribution to the public schools is a bit more than you had expected—but I . . ." (Cartoon by Dave Carpenter)

Gearing up for a Program of Individual Solicitation

Setting up a Local Educational Foundation (LEF)

One of the hottest fundraising trends in public education is to set up local educational foundations (LEFs) at either individual school sites or on a district-wide basis committed to achieving quality education for all children. The foundations are usually nonprofit (501c3) organizations that are tax-exempt third parties raising monies for the schools. They broaden the constituency and keep the community informed about the strengths and challenges of the schools. Local education foundations serve as independent third-party intermediaries on behalf of public education. They foster excellence in the schools by supporting innovative classroom practices and also provide assistance for students with special remedial needs. LEFs provide monies for equipment and services donated by generous businesses and individuals within the schools' community. Local education foundations in many parts of the country also sponsor competitive mini-grant programs for teachers.

Howie Schaffer, Managing Editor of the Public Education Network, a national association of local education funds based in Washington, DC, estimates that there were approximately 4,000 local educational foundations nationally in the year 2000 serving about 15 percent of schools.

When setting up a local education foundation, it is critical that it be done correctly. Make certain to consult with an attorney or a technical assistance agency whose staff has experience in this area. According to the California Consortium of Education Foundations (*http://www.cceflink.org*), there are ten basic steps that should be followed when forming a local education foundation:

- Establish a core leadership group
- Define your reason for being
- Share your plans with school and community leaders
- File for tax-exempt status
- Develop bylaws
- Recruit a board that reflects your community
- Establish committees and draft policies
- Develop a priority project list and an allocations process
- Create a fundraising plan and outline, identifying your unique resources
- Celebrate your success and evaluate your progress

A number of local education foundations around the country are becoming more astute and serious about their role as fundraisers. In some instances, executive directors have been employed to head up foundations and are providing fundraising leadership on a full-time basis. Additionally, some districts are employing full-time grant writers and fundraising consultants to assist in developing a comprehensive fundraising plan. Others have set up their own websites. While this new trend is worthwhile and helpful, the monies raised by local education foundations is only about .3 percent of a typical district's budget, according to the ERIC Clearinghouse on Educational Management.

Identifying Methods to Organize Both Annual and Capital Campaigns

Annual Campaigns   LEFs and other school fundraising groups focus primarily on annual campaigns to raise monies for the schools. Annual campaigns are ongoing yearly appeals that provide supplementary support. Gifts tend to be smaller than capital campaign gifts, which have loftier goals. New donors are solicited each year in an annual campaign and previous donors are courted to increase their contributions. Some of the fundraising approaches used in annual campaigns are: phonathons; direct mail solicitations and e-mail solicitations; auctions; telethons; public service announcements; electronic fundraising; dinner meetings, breakfast meetings, and luncheons; group meetings with Rotary, Kiwanis, PTA, and other groups; special events like golf tournaments and tennis tournaments; knocking on doors; and website solicitations including your own or other websites designed for this purpose. Also see the Bibliography to find out more about these approaches to raising monies on an annual basis.

Capital Campaigns   Capital campaigns have higher goals than annual campaigns and, because of this, gift requests are set far higher than annual appeals. Capital campaigns are very new to the public schools and some school districts are beginning to recognize this tremendous potential resource for external funding. Time frames in capital campaigns are generally extended, such as a three-year campaign or a five-year campaign, as opposed to a yearly campaign. Prospects are asked to

"Ms. Williams, the school board would like to see a copy of that speech you gave last night to those potential donors." (Cartoon by Dave Carpenter)

"pledge" a certain amount of money over time, such a three to five years. Capital campaigns are an exciting time in a school community because the goals are tangible and the results are highly visible. For example: A school district might need monies to build a creative and performing arts center. It decides to engage in a three-year capital campaign to raise monies for this purpose. The district first identifies someone in the community to make a "lead gift." This person might be motivated by an opportunity to have the facility named after his or her family. The conversation might go something like this: You suggest to Sam Jones, "I would like you to consider creating a new facility at the high school called, 'The Jones Family Performing Arts Center' that will cost approximately $10 million. We would like you to make the lead gift for $5 million for this purpose." This, of course, would be a source of great pride for the Jones family and possibly motivate the Jones's to make this exceptional contribution.

Funding opportunities for naming other portions of the performing arts center should be made available. Donors can receive public recognition for funding the seats, the stage, lighting, dressing rooms, and the main lobby. This is one of the reasons why capital campaigns have such great appeal to prospective donors and why they become motivated to make major contributions.

Named gifts, as described above, have been around for a long time on private school campuses, colleges, and universities, and nonprofit facilities like YMCAs, YWCAs, and Boys and Girls Clubs. The public schools should take a close look at this fundraising opportunity and realize that the schools are a wonderful place for a family to leave a lasting legacy by having a school building, ball field or seat in a little theater named after them. A step-by-step approach to individual solicitation of gifts is outlined below. More ideas and resources concerning this topic are listed in the Bibliography.

Trends in Giving

Based upon my own experience and the experience of others over the years, you might expect the following giving trends for both annual and capital campaigns. It should be noted that these trends are approximate and vary based upon the community in which you reside and the cause you represent.

Annual Campaigns

- About 60 percent of the monies come from 5 percent of the contributors
- About 40 percent of the monies comes from 95 percent of the contributors

If your annual campaign goal is to raise $100,000 and you had 100 contributors, then you might expect to receive $60,000 from five contributors for an average of $12,000 each and $40,000 from 95 contributors for an average of $421 each.

Capital Campaigns

■ One-third of the monies come from approximately 10 contributors
■ One-third of the monies come from approximately 100 contributors
■ One-third of the monies come from the rest of the contributors

If your goal is to raise $300,000 in a capital campaign, then you might expect to receive 10 contributions of $10,000 each; 100 contributions of $1,000 each; and, the remaining $100,000 from the rest of the contributors.

What are the implications of all this? First, look for a person in your constituency who will make a *key gift*. Once the key gift is made, start going after the other gifts. Second, understand that not all people in your constituency will make a contribution to your fundraising campaign. In fact, expect that approximately 10 to 20 percent of your constituents will make a gift to your cause. What is a key gift? Depending on the size of your campaign, a key gift could actually be of any denomination. For example: If you need $100,000 for your campaign, a key gift might be $10,000 to $20,0000. If you need $25,000, a key gift might be $2,500 to $5,000. If you need $1 million, a key gift might be $100,000 to $200,000.

A Step-by-Step Approach to Individual Solicitation of Gifts

■ There are many ways to solicit major gifts from prospects in your school community. The most desirable, but most difficult, way is to approach prospects individually. Because of the personal nature of this strategy and its importance to you and your cause, you should approach potential donors only after doing a significant amount of research on each person and his or her professional and personal background.

■ Solicitation on a person-to-person basis is the most effective way to raise serious dollars. There is an old adage that says, "People contribute money to people with causes and not just to causes." This is not to say that donors are not interested in causes, because they are, but it is the dynamics of a face-to-face meeting with someone who is a friend that helps snare the gift.

■ Before attempting to ask for monies from individuals, it is imperative that you study the materials in this book and also become familiar with the materials in the Bibliography. If monies are available, employ consultants who specialize in individual giving to help train staff and volunteers. Without study and training with someone who has been on the "firing line" and brought in thousands of dollars, you are probably doomed to failure. This is serious and demanding work but the payoff can be very rewarding.

■ Set aside a budget for individual solicitation of major gifts in your school or school district. The budget should include monies to employ a consultant (if you can) and for printing and duplication of materials.

■ Fundraising is a very competitive business and unless your campaign is considered a top priority item by prospective donors, your chances for success are doomed. Utilizing a group process technique, prepare a *case statement* of two to five pages in length that is clear, concise, and compelling. The case statement should indicate what you need the money for and highlight the staff's competence and ability to deliver. It is imperative that you include in the case statement the precise reason for your appeal, what you will achieve if your objectives are met, and the students and staff who will benefit. The case statement should be reproduced on good quality 8½" by 11" paper, or made into a "slick" multicolored brochure, depending on your budget. In either case, the content is more important than the format used for the statement. Prepare multiple copies of the statement for handout purposes, and train the staff and volunteers on how to use the materials to achieve maximum results.

■ Recruit volunteers in your community to work on a fundraising committee. Include, among others, prominent citizens who are well known and well thought of. Invite these people to an orientation meeting held by some of the key people in the school district, such as the superintendent, principals, board members, teachers, community leaders and others. Use a Power Point presentation or other powerful audiovisual means to communicate your message and highlight your cause. Answer all questions and concerns in a forthright and efficient manner. Ask participants to make a commitment of time and money before the meeting is concluded.

■ Make certain that the volunteers contribute their gift first before they approach prospective donors. This will help by providing them with "boasting rights" and will demonstrate to prospective donors that the cause is so worthy that the volunteers have already made contributions.

■ Utilizing the services of a good fundraising consultant, provide a comprehensive training program that involves role playing and videotaping (if possible). Use prepared scripts and prepared situations such as "overcoming objections," "asking for the gift," and "deciding how much to ask for." There are training programs available in some of resource materials listed in the Bibliography. The training program should be mandatory for all members of the fundraising committee.

■ Develop a prospective donors list in cooperation with the fundraising committee. Decide as a group how much you plan to ask each person to give. The committee should identify the names of wealthy parents, grandparents, teachers (including retired teachers), administrators, staff, friends, alumni (elementary, middle school, and high school), business people, politicians, other retirees, and others that reside in the constituency. Try to match up the list of prospective donors with people on the fundraising committee who might know any of the prospective donors as friends or acquaintances, and ask them to make the contact after they have gone through the training program.

■ Two people should approach a potential donor as a team. The team might include a principal and a volunteer, the superintendent and a volunteer, a board member and the superintendent, a teacher and a volunteer, or other groups of two. **Note:** In a situation where a major contributor has already made a gift to your cause and is interested in soliciting a friend to make another major gift, it is suggested that you encourage that a one-on-one solicitation take place between the major donor and his or her friend.

■ Appointments should be made and meetings should take place with prospective donors in a quiet, peaceful atmosphere not disturbed by telephone calls, interruptions, and extraneous conversation and noise. My first choice would be at the home or office of the potential donor. A second choice would be in a meeting room at the school or district office. I do not recommend luncheon or dinner meetings or meetings held in public places such as on the golf course or on the tennis court. Meetings at these locations have a tendency to get away from the business at hand. The major consideration is the comfort level of the prospect to be in an environment to discuss a gift. Remember, when you make an appointment to meet with a prospective donor, you are actually going on a *business call* to ask for the order.

■ Meetings with prospects should be arranged for no more than 30 to 45 minutes. If additional time is needed, let the prospect decide to extend the meeting.

■ If you do not know the prospects you are assigned to meet with, you must do research before the scheduled meeting. You must discover, if possible, their educational and business backgrounds, their financial backgrounds, their family backgrounds, the organizations to which they belong, their social affiliations, their interests and hobbies. You should also determine if any member of their family attended or is attending your district schools, if the potential donor is involved in any school activities or functions, and if the family has given monies to the schools in the past. Research where they have received their degrees and whether they sit on any important corporate boards. By doing comprehensive prospect research concerning each potential donor, your chances of receiving gifts increase substantially because you are connecting with the prospect in human terms.

■ When meeting with a potential donor make sure you "break the ice" by talking about areas of mutual interest that you have discovered in your prospect research. For example: If you are a tennis player and the potential donor is a tennis player, you might say something like, "I understand that you are a tennis player. How often do you play?" If you are a graduate of Harvard University and you discover that the potential donor is a graduate of Harvard, you might say, "I graduated from Harvard, or my dad graduated from Harvard. What was your major?"

■ The next step is to explain why you are meeting with the potential donor. This is a time to impress this person and discuss your cause. You might mention the outstanding staff that you have plus any additional staff that you intend to put into place. You should talk about the benefits and advantages of having this new and innovative program (or some other cause) and the how beneficial the program will be to the donor. Be sure to provide the prospect with a copy of the cause statement. When presenting your cause, you should listen aggressively and pay close attention to the potential donor. Watch for signs of approval or disapproval. Watch for body language that might be indicative of the comfort level of the prospect.

- Treat objections as questions the potential donor has rather than attacks on your program or credibility. Never let an objection lead to an argument. Always hear an objection out and respond with solutions. Convert the objection into an answerable question. You might say, "I realize that you are concerned about the district's reading program. Would you like to participate on the district's reading committee?" Finding common ground with the prospect is another way of turning negatives into positives. "I realize that our reading program can improve. This is why we are seeking your help." Make sure to identify honest objections and respond with facts. Do not make excuses and respond candidly to any questions asked. You might say, "I realize our reading scores went down this year in fifth grade, but did you know that our overall scores are still considerably higher than most school districts in the area?" Handle objections as they come up. Say, "I am delighted that you brought this matter up. I, too, do not like the fact that our scores went down." Finally, look at objections as questions that the potential donor has. If the prospect really had no intention of giving you a gift in the first place, he or she would not be meeting with you at all.

- When making the "big ask," always request a little more than you expect to receive and remain silent. It is critical to know how much to ask for, and this is decided after doing extensive prospect research. You might say, "We're hoping that you will consider an investment in our reading program by making a contribution of $50,000." Pause and let the request sink in and observe the prospect's behavior. Not asking for a large enough gift could lead to receiving a smaller gift than anticipated or not receiving a gift at all. People with money usually do not get upset if you ask them for more than they are considering. In fact, they might feel honored that you think they are more wealthy than they really are and surprise you with a gift that is larger than you expected.

- Do not accept a gift if you feel the gift is too small. It is better to make another appointment to further explore opportunities for giving a gift. You might say, "Let us leave the materials with you so you can study them and then we'll get together again in two weeks and answer any questions that you might have."

- If you receive a pledge from a prospect that you are happy with, express your appreciation enthusiastically and ask the person to complete and sign a pledge card. A sample pledge card is shown in the box on page 40. There are also software programs available that provide computerized pledge cards and accounting systems listed in the bibliography.

- Continue to cultivate those prospects that did not make a gift the first time they were approached and continue to seek out new prospects. Keep careful records for each prospect. Analyze why they did not make a pledge based upon your conversation with them, and go back again in three to six months. Also, you should maintain records for those people who did contribute to your cause so that you can return and ask for an additional gift that may be larger than the original gift.

Pledge Card
XYZ School District
100 Ferryboat Lane
Anywhere, USA
Computer Laboratory Fund Campaign

No. _____   Name _____ Date _____

Address _____

Telephone _____ e-mail _____

In consideration of the gifts of others and the obligations to be incurred based upon pledges received from the undersigned and others, I/we promise to pay the XYZ School District, Computer Laboratory Fund Campaign, the sum of

_____ dollars $ _____

X_____ _____
              Signature   Date

Please remind me _____ Annually _____ Semi-Annually _____ Quarterly

For _____ years ending _____ Month _____ Day _____ Year

- -

No. _____ Category/Division: _____ Volunteer: _____

Evaluation: _____ Pledge: _____ Project _____

Remarks: _____

_____

_____

■ Do not forget to acknowledge all those people who contributed to your fundraising campaign by sending them personal thank-you notes. The volunteers can help you with this task. Also, do not forget to recognize the volunteers themselves by thanking them publicly at a luncheon or dinner celebration. For major gift givers, you might want to have the superintendent personally thank these people at a "black-tie" reception. By doing all of these things, you are helping to ensure that all these participants will continue to support your programs into the future.

What Is Planned Giving?

Planned giving refers to the process of making a charitable gift of cash or noncash assets to one or more nonprofit organizations, including the public schools. The gift, when made, usually requires consideration and planning in light of the donor's overall estate plan. Legal documents to be completed should be made part of the overall estate plan of the donor. Because of the size and potential impact of such gifts, a donor should consult with his or her professional advisors before completing the process.

There are many tax advantages to giving cash and noncash assets to a nonprofit organization such as a school or a local education foundation. Giving noncash assets may be attractive to supporters of the schools in that they are donating to a good cause, and there are favorable tax implications for this kind of gift. Examples of appreciated assets are:

1. Stocks
2. Bonds
3. Shares in mutual funds
4. A home or farm property
5. Vacant land
6. Vacation or rental property
7. Commercial property
8. Other assets held in a form other than in cash

Property that has increased in value and has been owned on a long-term basis generally brings the most in tax savings for the donor. People also find that giving noncash property also leaves their cash available for other purposes. Most long-term appreciated property is deductible for its full fair market value when the gift is made to a charitable organization or a school. In addition, capital gains tax is not due on property that is donated rather than sold. Under current law, gifts of appreciated property worth up to 30 percent of the donor's adjusted gross income can be deducted in the year of the gift and excess deductions may be carried over into as many as the next five years if deductions are itemized. There are many ways to make gifts of appreciated and marketable securities and real property to the schools that provide significant tax advantages for the donor. Of course, gifts of cash are always welcome. The next section discusses noncash gifts and presents an explanation of gifts of cash that could be given to schools outright or bequeathed upon the death of the donor. In either case, a tax attorney or other certified accountant should be consulted before any transfer of ownership is made.

*Possible Gift Ideas for the Public Schools**

Appreciated Marketable Securities

One of the most attractive methods for givers to realize their charitable intentions toward the schools is in giving appreciated marketable securities. A gift of listed stocks, bonds, or other publicly traded securities entitles

---

*All information pertaining to tax benefits listed above is subject to change. Federal and state tax laws change on a continuing basis. In working with potential donors, encourage them to talk with their accountants and/or tax attorneys concerning any of the above. Accompany them, if they so desire, to discuss their objectives and the opportunities available to them. For a more complete discussion of individual solicitation see also publications listed in the Bibliography.

the giver to a charitable income tax deduction equal to the full fair market value of the securities on the date of the gift, provided that the securities were owned for at least one year. In addition, the donor does not incur capital gains tax on the transfer of such securities to the schools.

Entire Interest in Real Estate

An outright gift of unencumbered real estate may enable the giver to make a significant gift to the schools without incurring capital gains tax on the transfer of the appreciated asset. The gift will entitle the giver to a charitable income tax deduction equal to the fair market value of the interest in the property on the date of the transfer, provided that the property was owned for more than one year.

Remainder Interest in Certain Types of Real Property

A *charitable remainder trust* is a unique gift opportunity available to people who own a primary residence, a second home, or a farm and wish to dispose of such property in their estate, but want to continue using the property for their lifetime. They may give the schools a remainder interest in their property, retain the property for the rest of their lives, and receive income for the rest of their lives.

Tangible Personal Property

A person might wish to consider making a gift of personal property such as art objects, books, and other collectibles to the schools. If the schools can use and are expected to use the gift of such property toward the furtherance of the educational mission and the property has been owned for more than one year, the giver will be eligible for a fair market value charitable income tax deduction without having to recognize the capital gain on any appreciation and will receive a tax credit for the fair market value of the property.

Life Insurance

If a person owns a life insurance policy and no longer requires its protection, he or she may wish to consider transferring ownership of the policy to the schools. Another possibility is to purchase a new policy and transfer ownership to the schools. Each gift will generate a charitable income tax deduction roughly equal to the cash surrender value of the policy on the date of the gift.

Cash

An outright gift of cash for some people is the most comfortable gift to give. It is also very much appreciated by the recipient organization in that cash is easy to administer and can be used for multiple purposes. Many people give cash gifts to worthy causes and are more comfortable in giving in this manner. Sometimes people have a specific cause to which they want to contribute and will so designate. This is referred to as a *restrictive gift.* Others will give cash and not place any restrictions on how the money is spent. This is considered an *unrestrictive gift.* Needless to say, unrestrictive gifts offer more flexibility than restrictive gifts. However, any gifts of cash are always appreciated.

Assignment

Individual Solicitation

1. Locate a wealthy person in your community.
2. Do prospect research to obtain relevant information that would assist you if you were assigned to solicit monies from this person.
3. Estimate how much money you would ask for if you were part of a team of two people soliciting a gift.
4. What information would you highlight in your meeting with the prospect?
5. Meet in groups of three to five persons to discuss and share your findings. Keep your prospect anonymous.

BIBLIOGRAPHY

Books and Periodicals

1. Barrett, Richard D., & Molly E. Ware. *Planned Giving Essentials: A Step by Step Guide to Success.* Aspen Publishers, P.O. Box 990, Frederick, MD 21705. Provides an introduction to the essentials of planned giving and explains how to set up a planned giving program. Provides sample estate and annuity agreements and IRS forms for gifts of personal property. Tel: (800) 638-8437

2. Burnett, Ken. *Friends for Life: Relationship Fundraising in Practice.* Precept Press, 160 East Illinois Street, Chicago, IL 60611. Examines nonprofits and what they have done to improve donor relations. Tel: (312) 467-0424

3. L. Peter Edles. *Fundraising Hands-on Tactics for Nonprofit Groups.* McGraw-Hill, Inc., New York. A step-by-step approach through the logic and practical application of organizing, developing, and conducting membership and constituent fundraising drives. Actual training examples are provided.

4. *Kiplinger Magazine,* September 2000, p. 117–121. "Charity Gets Personal." Washington, DC. Innovative giving methods are discussed allowing new philanthropists to attack fundamental problems including giving with others, creating their own donor-advised fund, mutual funds that offer charitable programs, gifts that give back, and the bright future for fundraising.

5. Kuniholm, Roland. *The Complete Book of Model Fund-Raising Letters.* Prentice Hall, Paramus, NJ 07652. Over 350 sample and model letters to generate higher donations for any nonprofit organization.

6. Kushner, Barbara-Ciconte, & Jeanne G. Jacob. *Fund Raising Basics: A Complete Guide.* Aspen Publishers, P.O. Box 990, Frederick, MD 21705. Discusses annual giving, direct-mail fund raising, major gifts, special events, capital campaigns, prospect research, technology, and others. Tel: (800) 638-8437

7. Landsdowne, David. *The Relentlessly Practical Guide to Raising Serious Money.* Emerson and Church, P.O. Box 336, Medfield, MA 02052-0336. Provides

assistance on ways to solicit major gifts, planned gifts, donations to capital campaigns, direct mail solicitation, special events, and telemarketing. Tel: (508) 359-0019

8. McCormick, Dan H., David G. Bauer, & Daryl E. Ferguson. *Creating Foundations for American Schools.* Aspen Publishers, Inc., 200 Orchard Ridge Drive, Gaithersburg, MD 20878. New resource provides the know-how necessary to set up your foundation and keep it running smoothly. Includes sample documents, tax forms, guide to laws and more. *www.aspenpublishers.com*

9. Moerschbaecher, Lynda S. *Starting at Square One: Starting and Managing the Planned Gift Program.* Precept Press, 160 East Illinois Street, Chicago, IL 60611. Guide to starting a planned giving program that explains how to assess current sources of revenue, determine the appropriate size for a planned giving program, develop policies, and make the pitch to the board of trustees. Also shows how to tie planned giving into a capital campaign, use consultants, understand the tax laws that govern planned gifts, market the program to potential donors, and avoid conflicts of interest. Tel: (800) 225-3775

10. Muro, James J. *Creating and Funding Educational Foundations.* Allyn & Bacon, 75 Arlington Street, Boston, MA. 02116. A comprehensive guide to creating and operating a private educational foundation for local school districts. Provides descriptions of various fundraising techniques such as annual fund drives, direct-mail and telephone fundraising, personal solicitation, raising funds from foundations, and raising funds with special events.

11. National Committee on Planned Giving. *The Journal of Gift Planning,* 233 McCrea Street, Suite 400, Indianapolis, IN 46225. Published quarterly, this magazine discusses techniques for fund raisers who specialize in deferred gifts and the laws that regulate planned giving. Tel: (317) 269-6276

12. G. Roger Shoenfels, Publisher, *Planned Giving Today,* 100 Second Avenue South, Suite 180, Edmonds, WA 98020. Professional newsletter that serves the charitable gift-planning community as a practical resource for education, information, inspiration, and professional linkage. Tel: (800) 525-5748

13. The Taft Group. *Practical Guide to Planned Giving 2000* (8th ed.). P.O. Box 9187, Farmington Hills, MI 48333-9187. Experts explain new trends in planned giving, regulatory changes, and methods of solicitation; discuss how to start and manage a planned-giving program; and provide overviews of tax considerations and various kinds of annuities and trusts. Includes a bibliography of resources, a glossary of terms, tax forms and schedules, marketing tips, and the codes of ethics of four national fund-raising associations. Tel: (800) 877-4253

14. *Time* magazine, July 24, 2000, p. 49–59. "The New Philanthropists." New York, NY. Discusses new philanthropy in relationship to the giving habits of many of the new multimillionaires in the United States.

15. Underwood, Cliff. *Demystifying the Ask.* Underwood and Associates, 11835 Carmel Mountain Rd., San Diego, CA 92128. A handout used to accompany a comprehensive talk on individual solicitation including ladder of effectiveness, record keeping, doing your homework, closing techniques, asking for the gift, and overcoming objections. Tel: (858) 672-3224

Software

1. **CornerStone 2000.** Helps small nonprofit organizations manage donor and giving information, generate personalized letters and receipts, process gifts, and track fundraising efforts. Donor Automation, 912 New York Street, Redlands, CA 92374. Tel: (909) 793-4434. Website: *http://www.donor.com*

2. **DB-Cultivator.** Helps manage information on donors and keep track of pledges, special events, committees, major gifts, and direct mail. Generates personalized letters, labels, and reports. Oaktree Systems, 4462 Middle Country Road, Calverton, NY 11933. Tel. (800) 726-8163. Website: *http://oaktreesys.com*

3. **Denari 2000.** Keeps track of information on donors, volunteers, pledges, and gifts; and generates receipts, tax statements, and thank-you letters. Modules that provide fund accounting, track special events, and incorporate new mailing rules are also available. Synergy Development Systems, 11440 Okeechobee Boulevard, Suite 206, Royal Palm Beach, FL 33411. Tel: (800) 352-0312. Website: *http://www.denarisoft.com*

4. **DonorWorks 6.0.** Helps nonprofit groups maintain data on current and prospective donors and volunteers, manage special events, create personalized receipts and letters, and generate fundraising reports and charts. Users can electronically store photographs in donor records. StafSoft Technologies, P.O. Box 10010, Spokane, WA 99209-1010. Tel. (800) 414-7990. Website: *http://www.starsoft.com*

5. **Exceed.** Allows non-profit organizations to maintain information on donors, record pledges and gifts, track contacts with foundations and corporate giving programs, and generate fundraising reports. Additional modules available for direct mail and volunteer programs and as an interface with accounting software. Technology Resource Assistance Center, 610 Cowper Street, Palo Alto, CA 94301. Tel. (800) 676-5831. Website: *http://www.tracworld.com*

Some Relevant Websites

The following websites are provided to assist you in your search for grants and gifts for pre-K–12 schools. The content of the sites will broaden your perspective and make you more astute in asking for funding for your cause. You will become familiar with some of the professional organizations that are available to you, as well as those organizations that do extensive research in the field. Additionally, you will find some websites that offer consultant help.

Resource	*Web Address*
American Association of Fundraising Counsel	http://www.aafrc.org
Association of Fundraising Professionals	http://www.nsfre.org/
Carlton and Company	http://Findit.Org/html/ fund_raising.html
Chronicle of Philanthropy	http://philanthropy.com
Foundation Center	http://www.fdncenter.org
Kintera (Internet Fundraising)	http://www.kinterathon.com
Levenson and Associates	http://www.grantsandgiftsfor schools.com
National Association of Philanthropic Planners	http://www.napp.net
National Center for Charitable Statistics	http://www.urbanorg/data.htm
National Committee on Planned Giving	http://www.ncpg.org

Resource	**Web Address**
Parents Planet (Internet Fundraising)	http://parents-planet.com
Planned Giving Today	http://www.pgtoday.com
PTO Today (Internet Fundraising)	http://ptotoday.com
The Taft Group	http://www.taftgroup.com
Urban Institute	http://www.urban.org
Zimmerman—Lehman	http://www.zimmerman-lehman.com

4

How to Write A Grant Application

Part 1

In this chapter you will

❑ Distinguish between writing a government grant and writing a corporate and foundation grant

❑ Identify the six basic components of a grant application

❑ Learn how to gather needs assessment documentation

❑ Distinguish between goals and objectives

❑ Practice writing measurable objectives

❑ Learn what activities are and how to write them

Distinguishing between Writing a Government Grant and Writing a Corporate and Foundation Grant

Writing a government grant application is typically very time consuming. There are more forms to fill out, more sign-off sheets, more attachments, more assurances pages, more detailed budget pages, and more pages allotted to the program narrative than corporate and foundation grant applications. This translates into significant amounts of time needed to gather the data, write the narrative, and obtain the required signatures on the sign-off sheets. Some school districts have full-time grantwriters who coordinate this effort. Others hire outside consultants to assist in the government grant-writing effort or provide release time for teachers to complete the application. If help is available, you should welcome it. If help is not available, this chapter will provide you with the background and resources needed to write government grants as well as corporate and foundation grants. If you learn how to write a government grant, you will be able to write most grant applications that are out there, including state, corporate, and foundation grants.

In this chapter, you will become familiar and practice writing the six basic components of a grant application. You will also practice writing a minigrant utilizing a grant application format that would be applicable for most corporate, foundation, and government grants.

In Chapter 2 you learned that most corporate and foundation grant applications require just two to ten pages. Others require a one- to two-page letter of application. Nevertheless, if you learn how to prepare and write each section of a grant application and then learn how to assemble them into a complete grant application package, you will be prepared to compete for both large and small grants.

"Since your last idea really bombed, Harris, you won't be getting one of those little 'Idea Pads.'" (Cartoon by Dave Carpenter)

The Basic Components of a Grant Application

Most grant applications require the same six basic components:

1. Needs Assessment
2. Goals
3. Objectives
4. Activities (Methods)
5. Evaluation Specification (covered in Chapter 5)
6. Budget (covered in Chapter 5)

These components are interrelated as illustrated in the diagram below.

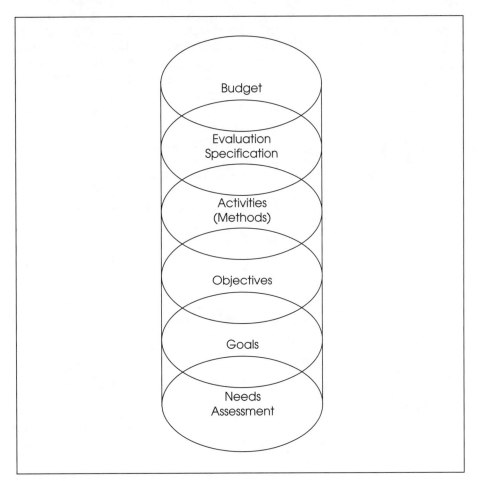

Needs Assessment

The needs assessment, stated in the beginning of the grant application, analyzes the extent of the problem and the conditions you wish to change. The statement of the problem or need is a representation of the reason for your proposal. It should demonstrate a clear understanding of the need in human terms and community benefits and should reinforce your credibility for investigating the problem. Adequate time should be devoted to reviewing the literature on the subject, including citing relevant research to justify why the problem should be investigated.

The needs statement should coincide with the interests and priorities of the funding agency. If the interests of the funding agency do not coincide with your needs, apply to another agency that has the same interests as yours. Do not waste your time or the funding agency's time if there is not a match up of your needs and the funding agency's priorities or interests. Doing your homework to determine funding agency's priorities and areas of interest, including grade-level interests, will save significant amounts of time, frustration, and energy and will increase your chances for success. This includes gathering information from funding agencies' websites, including the U.S. Department of Education, your state department of education, corporations, foundations, and others. Requesting relevant literature and publications on current grant opportunities from program officers and other contact people is also very helpful. Also, researching publications that announce grant opportunities on a continuing basis—such as *Education Funding News, Education Grants Alert, Chronicle of Philanthropy, Federal Grants and Contracts Weekly*, and *Foundation and Corporate Grants Alert*—will provide you with relevant, timely information concerning grant opportunities.

The first step in doing a comprehensive needs assessment is to define the general nature of the problem in a clear and concise manner. This is the most important step and should include the following.

Defining the General Nature of the Problem

■ Who has the problem?

■ How important and significant is the problem?

■ What is causing the problem?

■ What factors are presently aggravating the problem?

■ Why should the problem be of special interest to the funding agency?

When gathering your needs assessment documentation, involve the total school community. This includes students, teachers, parents, administrators, and other stakeholders. Describe the needs in human terms. An example of a population with specific need might be "the numbers of children who are limited and non-English speakers." In so doing, you will connect with the reader and make a more compelling statement. There are two types of data that you will be gathering: *hard data* and *soft data*.

Gathering Hard Data   Hard data is sometimes referred to as "cognitive data" and includes specific numbers and percentages gathered about topic such as grade levels, schools, ethnic makeup, gender, test scores, numbers of limited and non-English speakers, languages spoken in the home, education levels of parents and people in the community. Also, absenteeism; expulsions; juvenile delinquency; truancy; crime; divorce; vandalism; alcohol, tobacco, and drug use can be used. Additionally, socioeconomic levels, numbers of children on free or reduced lunch programs, transiency rates, geographic location, average size and ages of family members, unemployment rates, poverty levels, number of single parent households, and number of unwed mothers are all examples of hard data.

Gathering Soft Data * Soft data is sometimes referred to as "affective data" and may provide information on attitudes, values, feelings, and self-concepts of a select population. The information is usually gathered through observations, surveys, interviews, and anecdotal records. For example: If you wanted to find out about student attitudes toward reading in ability groups, then you might want to develop an interview schedule to measure how the students feel about this grouping method for reading. If you want to find out how parents feel about not having computers in the home, then you could develop a questionnaire to determine their feelings and send it home for completion. Observation checklists are also used to gather soft data about a particular classroom, subject area, or child. These checklists are usually developed by an external evaluator or curriculum specialist in cooperation with individual classroom teachers.

The box on page 52 contains a hypothetical example of how a needs assessment is reported in an application for federal assistance for a preschool program. The data can be expanded or cut back depending on the needs and desires of the funding agency.

Assignment 1

Needs Assessment

Think about a program in your school or school district that you would like to obtain monies for. Do not concern yourself with cost at this time. Using the Mini-Grant Program Application appearing on pages 71–73, go directly to section 3.0, Needs Assessment Documentation. Over the next week, begin to gather data for this section of the application including both hard data and soft data. Once you complete this section, duplicate your work and be prepared to distribute it to a group of three to five persons assigned to your group. Answer the following questions in the group:

1. What techniques did you use to gather the needs assessment data?
2. Were you able to review relevant literature on the web and cite research findings to justify why the problem should be investigated?
3. Were you able to gather both hard data and soft data?
4. What suggestions does the group have for improving your needs assessment section of the application?

---

*It should be pointed out that gathering soft data is sometimes considered controversial because of the personal nature of the questions asked. It is recommended that all instrumentation designed for this purpose should first be approved by the school principal and then by the parents before administering to the students.

XYZ School District

Example of Needs Assessment Documentation for a Preschool Program

The XYZ School District, located in XYZ City, XYZ State, encompasses preschool through grade 12 in fifteen schools serving approximately 9,300 students. More than 90 percent of the students are from minority groups and more than 75 percent are Hispanic. With an ethnically diverse population of approximately 100,000 and an average income that is less than half the national average, the XYZ School District ranks as one of the poorest urban districts in both the state and country. The median income for XYZ City last year was $26,000, adjusted for inflation. Thirty percent of the families of students attending schools in XYZ School District are on Aid to Families with Dependent Children (AFDC). Single parents account for 59 percent of the households and 38 percent of that figure are female heads of household with children. Sixty percent of the female heads of households live below the federal poverty level. Over 40 percent of the XYZ City's adult population lacks a high school diploma, and 50 percent of the families move at least once a year.

The XYZ School District has a total of 4,767 limited English proficient students. Overall, the district ranks 35th in the entire state in the numbers of limited English proficient students as a percentage of enrollment. Standardized test scores for the district indicate overall that students are below state norms in reading, writing, and mathematics.

XYZ School, the target site for the Preschool Program, is located on the east side of the school district and has an overall preschool through 6th grade population of 750 students, of which 92 percent are minority and 55 percent are limited English proficient. The Child Development Center, located at XYZ School, provides day care services to 75 preschool-aged children from low-income families in a state-subsidized program. The Center has a waiting list of 415 children. Ninety percent of the families served at the Child Development Center fall below the state poverty level and do not pay a fee.

Last year, a community needs assessment was conducted to help identify the health and social service needs of the XYZ School residents and to identify service inconsistencies. A broad-based participation survey was utilized that included input from parents, community members, agency workers, educators, and others. Sixty families were randomly selected to represent the school's ethnic and socioeconomic diversity. They were administered intensive one-on-one in-depth interviews in their dominant language. After the sixty families identified key areas of need, more than thirty-five community members participated in open forums, which were held at the school site to assist in prioritizing and expanding the identified needs. Focus groups, including personnel from health, educational, and social service agencies also provided input on community needs and barriers to existing services. The focus groups were organized in six different categories including public agencies, elementary and secondary schools, law enforcement, emergency services, mental health agencies, and community service agencies. The following needs were identified as being most critical to the school:

- Strengthened partnerships and relationships between parents, teachers, community members, and others regarding the preschool needs of children at XYZ School
- Strengthened partnerships with XYZ School staff related to parent education programs
- Ability for parents to access health and social service information at the XYZ School site

Goals

Goals are general in nature, broad-based, and overarching. They summarize what you want to accomplish in your grant application. It is recommended that you state one to four goals in each application. People oftentimes confuse goals with objectives when asked to write objectives by the funding agency. It is important to be able to distinguish between the two. Once you understand the differences, you will not confuse them.

Some Examples of Goals

1. To have all students work at grade level in mathematics in grades 1-6.
2. To support parents, including mothers, fathers, and guardians in their role as primary caregivers and educators of their children.
3. To provide a comprehensive two-way bilingual education program that includes listening, speaking, reading, and writing.
4. To develop a highly trained, competent, and caring staff in the science and math departments of the high school.
5. To introduce Microsoft Word to middle school students in grades 6 through 8.

Objectives

Program (outcome) objectives specify the "outcomes" of your project—the end product. Each objective is related to the goal and is directly related to the needs statement. Program objectives are measurable and time-specific and become the criteria by which the effectiveness of your program is evaluated. They define the population to be served in numerical terms and are quantifiable. Sometimes referred to as "product objectives" or "behavioral objectives," they are very important in the eyes of the project readers in that they are at the "heart" of the project and are directly related to the needs assessment. Program objectives are more specific than goals. They do not describe the activities or methods. When agencies fund your project, they are actually buying your objectives. When evaluators evaluate your project, they are measuring whether you accomplished what you said you were going to do in your program objectives.

When writing program objectives that are quantifiable, you are usually taking something negative and making it positive. Program objectives state such things as: "to increase," "to decrease," "to reduce," "to be able to" within a specified amount of time. For example: "to increase reading comprehension skills at least one month for each month of instruction as measured by _____." It is essential to write clear, concise, measurable program objectives, or you will probably not get funded. To be useful, program objectives should:

- Tell who is going to be doing what
- Tell when it is going to take place
- Describe how much change will be taking place
- Tell how it is going to be measured

Understanding How to Write Process Objectives   Process objectives are measurable and are written to assist in ensuring that the program objectives are achieved. They are not program objectives and they do not identify outcomes related to learning. Instead, process objectives support program objectives and are essential to providing for smooth program implementation. When writing process objectives, state such things as: "to provide," "to establish," "to create," "to schedule," "to assist," "to observe," "to meet," "to visit." For example: "to establish a Community Learning Center as of September 15 as measured by records available at the school office and verified by parent participants."

Some Additional Examples

Program (Outcome) Objectives

1. At the conclusion of the project period, at least 80 percent of the target students will be able to increase their understanding of science concepts for their grade level as measured by a district-developed science rubric.
2. At the conclusion of the project period, at least 90 percent of the target students will express positive attitudes about the mathematics program for their grade level as measured by "pre" and "post" attitude surveys developed by the mathematics department.
3. At the conclusion of the project period, at least 80 percent of the target students will be able to demonstrate increased growth at the .05 level or better in district reading and language arts assessments, as measured by standardized tests for their grade levels.
4. At the conclusion of the project period, at least 80 percent of the target students will gain at least one month academically for each month of instruction in reading comprehension and reading vocabulary as measured by a standardized test.

Process Objectives

1. The school counselor will meet with each program participant at least once a week beginning on October 1 as measured by logs kept by each counselor.
2. The project will provide thirty laptop computers beginning in September for students to take home as measured by school records kept on file in the project director's office.
3. Each student participant will visit the school media center at least twice a week for twelve weeks beginning in October to do research and report back on the Civil War as measured by records kept by the school librarian and the classroom teacher.
4. A Parent Advisory Group of twenty-five parents will be established by September 15 and meet at least once a month as measured by logs kept by the Community Facilitator.

Assignment 2

Goals And Objectives

1. Using the Mini-Grant Program Application on pages 71–73, insert in the section marked "GOAL" one overall goal for your project for which you have already gathered needs assessment documentation.
2. Begin to write at least five program (outcome) objectives and at least five process objectives in the section marked "OBJECTIVES." Use additional sheets if needed.
3. Number your objectives 1.0, 2.0, 3.0, 4.0, and so on. Under 1.0, you can add additional numbers if related and necessary by indenting and adding 1.1, 1.2, 1.3 and so on. See example on page 72.
4. Provide copies of your goals and objectives for your working group of three to five persons. Critique this section for each member in the group, answering the following questions:
   - Is the goal that is written overarching and general in nature?
   - Are all the objectives measurable?
   - Are the objectives specifically related to the needs assessment?
   - Do the objectives state how and when they are going to be evaluated?
   - Do you have suggestions for improvement of the objectives?

Activities

The activities (methods) section explains in detail how you are going to achieve the desired outcomes stated in your objectives. Activities explain what will be done, who will do it, and when it will get done. Activities should be well thought out and related to each objective. The activities section should include a description of program staffing and the students to be served, as well as the rationale for selecting the students. It should flow smoothly from the needs statement and the program objectives. Several activities are usually presented for each objective.

The activity section in your application should answer the following questions:

■ What are you going to do to meet the objectives of the project?

■ What are the projected starting and ending dates?

■ Who is going to be responsible to coordinate, direct, and evaluate the project?

■ What kinds of facilities, materials, equipment, and capital improvements will be needed to implement the project?

■ How will the participants and staff be selected?

■ Who will be responsible to complete each activity?

■ What evidence do you have that the rationale for the activities selected is going to yield positive results? (Refer to research findings, expert opinion, and past experience with similar programs)

■ Who will be responsible to ensure that the activities presented are reflected in the budget request?

A hypothetical example of an Activities Component for an Academy of the Arts project is displayed in the following box.

Blue Danube Academy of the Arts

Sample of Activities Flowing from Objectives

OBJECTIVE ONE: 90 percent of the middle school students participating in the Blue Danube Academy of the Arts dance program will be able to satisfactorily focus attention on kinesthetic awareness in responding to a variety of stimuli and perform specific and repeatable movement sequences taught by the instructor as measured by teacher observation and an external evaluator.

ACTIVITIES:

- 100 students will be selected for this program based upon interest, artistic talent, motivation, parent interest, and referrals from classroom teachers.
- 5 dance teachers will be employed based upon their experience and training in working with middle school students.
- Academy dance classes will be held after school, during intersession, and during summer school.
- No tuition fees will be charged.
- Each class will be scheduled for six weeks.
- Students will be taught kinesthetic awareness exercises for dance, including musical beats and rhythms.
- Students will be taught how to manipulate forces and qualities of movement through active participation in dance and rhythms.
- Students will be asked to demonstrate the ability to rework dances as a result of class discussion, videotaping, peer responses, and self-evaluation.
- Teachers will be asked to complete an internal evaluation of the after-school program every three weeks.
- An external evaluator will be asked to do an external evaluation of the total program and provide a written evaluation to the administration and to the funding source.
- Program is revised and then recycles after six weeks.

For most proposals, it is a good idea to include a timeline to show when the activities will be carried out and who is responsible for carrying out each activity. I recommend using a Triple "T" Chart (Task, Time, Talent) for this purpose. An example of a Triple "T" Chart related to a health education program is shown on page 57.

Example of a Timeline Using a Triple "T" Chart

XYZ School District

Health Education Grant for Development of Curriculum Materials

Task	Time	Talent
1. Form Curriculum Development Advisory Group (CDAG)	7-1	Principal* Parents Teachers Community Groups
2. Hire Health Education Consultant and Curriculum Development Team	8-1	Principal* CDAG
3. Begin to develop curriculum packets	8-15	Health Education Consultant* Curriculum Development Team
4. Begin staff development program	9-15	(Same as 3)
5. Begin field testing curriculum materials	10-1	(Same as 3)
6. Revise curriculum materials	11-1	(Same as 3)
7. Conduct home visitation program	11-15 through 4-15	Parent Educators*
8. Complete internal evaluation of program	5-1	Principal* CDAG Staff
9. Complete external evaluation of program	6-1	External Evaluator*
10. Revise and recycle for year two	8-1	Health Education Consultant* Curriculum Development Team

*Person primarily responsible to complete task

Assignment 3

Activities Section

1. Using the Mini-Grant Program Application on pages 71–73 write at least five activities for each objective that you wrote in the objectives section. Place the activities into the "ACTIVITIES" section of the mini-grant application.
2. Number the activities to correspond to the numbering system of each objective. See examples on pages 71–73.
3. Distribute copies of the activities section to class/workshop groups.
4. Critique the activities section in relationship to each objective and make suggestions for improvement.

5

How to Write A Grant Application

Part II

In this chapter you will

☐ Learn how to organize and write an evaluation plan

☐ Be able to put together a budget and a budget justification

☐ Learn helpful hints to improve your chances of getting funded

☐ Write a mini-grant

The Evaluation Plan

The evaluation plan determines the extent to which the objectives of your project are met and the activities carried out. It should demonstrate the effectiveness of your program and provide assistance to you in those areas that need improvement. Based upon the results of the evaluation, you can better allocate resources, improve your program offerings, and improve the overall effectiveness of your program. By completing a comprehensive evaluation of your program and making necessary changes for improvement, your chances for additional funding in ensuing years becomes easier. If you have written measurable objectives and activities that are related to each objective, then it should be easy to write the evaluation plan.

There are two types of evaluations that are used in writing the evaluation component for your grant proposal. These are *internal evaluation* and *external evaluation*, sometimes referred to as *formative* and *summative evaluation*.

Internal (Formative) Evaluation

An internal or formative evaluation deals primarily with self-assessment as related to the proposed project. It addresses questions about implementation and ongoing planning related to the overall program. This could include a self-assessment of the teaching-learning process, the school, the school district, and the school community. It is a structured way for the teachers, the staff, the administration, the parents, the school community, and the school board to assess progress and make changes in ways that lead to greater achievement of the goals and objectives of the program.

Evaluation is looked upon as an ongoing process. Information gathered should be shared internally and externally to assist in making individual and collective decisions that move your classroom, your school, or school district to new levels of excellence. Internal evaluation should be ongoing, nonthreatening, asking good questions, collecting information, sharing information, and making decisions to achieve organizational effectiveness. In projects under $5,000, an internal evaluation should be sufficient; however, some funding agencies might prefer that you also include an external evaluation.

External (Summative) Evaluation

While an internal evaluation is a positive force for change and empowerment, there are many funding agencies that look favorably upon, or require, an external or summative evaluation report. The external or summative evaluation report showcases outcomes associated with your program and offers suggestions for improvement. These agencies believe that an external evaluator will assure a candid and unbiased assessment of the project, will have knowledge and expertise in data gathering techniques and instrumentation, and will report the findings in a clear and concise manner. I like to include an external evaluation of all my grant applications over $5,000, whether the funding agency requires it or not. I believe that employing an external evaluator is a positive step in getting your project approved for funding.

Some school districts employ an evaluation consultant to assist them in writing the evaluation plan. While this approach is positive, caution should be exercised if the consultant eventually becomes the external evaluator. You want to be absolutely certain that this person will not be biased in providing you with an honest, fair, and candid assessment of your program.

More emphasis is being placed on the evaluation plan and the evaluation results than ever before. Funding agencies and wealthy individuals giving money to worthy causes want to be assured that their monies will be well spent. It is essential that you prepare a comprehensive evaluation plan that is clear, concise and well thought out.

Questions to Respond to When Writing the Evaluation Plan   When writing the evaluation plan, make certain that you respond to the following questions:

- Are you presenting a clear strategy for evaluating program objectives and activities (methods)?
- Are you specifying who will be evaluated, what will be evaluated, how many participants will be evaluated, and how participants will be chosen?
- Are you explaining when the evaluation will take place?
- Are you describing the design, instrumentation, and methods to be used to collect the data?
- Are you specifying who will be responsible for completing the evaluation and reporting the results?
- Are you indicating how the results of the evaluation will be used for program refinement, revision and improvement?

Presenting a Clear Strategy for Evaluating Program Objectives and Activities. If the objectives written are measurable and the activities describe how you are going to achieve the objectives, then it will be easy to present a clear and meaningful strategy for evaluating the program. In fact, most of the evaluation component will have been written if you do a good job with your objectives and activities. Developing a Triple "T" Chart will also assist you in presenting a clear strategy for evaluating program objectives and activities.

Describing Who, What, and How Many Participants Will Be Chosen. This section is one of the most important elements of your evaluation plan. Funding agencies base a lot of their budgetary decisions on this data. For example, projects involving many schools, many students, and many teachers cost more to implement than projects involving fewer schools, students, and teachers. These types of projects also impact more students than other projects. The funding agency needs to have this information to make a funding decision. Providing a realistic budget request in relationship to the size and scope of the project will help your chances of getting funded.

Explaining When the Evaluation Will Take Place. Explaining when the evaluation will take place and publishing the plan for all to see is essential. Is the evaluation going to include pre- and post-testing? If so, when will this testing take place? In addition, will there be continuous testing by classroom teachers? Will there be observations, questionnaires, or interviews? When will the testing take place? As mentioned above, if your objectives and activities are described properly and you develop a Triple "T" Chart, then this section will not be difficult to write.

Describing the Design, Implementation and Methods to Be Used to Collect the Data. If your project is under $5,000 and your school plans to do its evaluation, be certain to describe your evaluation plan as clearly and succinctly as you can. First, take a look at the overall project. Study the goals, objectives, and activities. If the objectives written are truly measurable, then it should not be difficult to evaluate each objective. Describe your design succinctly, tell how you are going to implement the project, and include the methods that you will use to collect and report the data.

If your project is over $5,000 and the needs demand a more sophisticated evaluation design, including identification of instrumentation and data gathering techniques, you might want to consider employing an external evaluator for the project. Many school districts ask the external evaluator or an evaluation consultant to assist them in writing the evaluation component for their project. As mentioned above, caution should be exercised when employing the same person to write the evaluation component for the project who will also serve as the external evaluator.

When employing an external evaluator, ask for a biographical sketch to be placed into the appendix of the application and include examples of surveys, questionnaires, data gathering instruments, data analysis forms, and other relevant materials that will be used. This lends credibility and strength to your request for funding.

Specifying Who Will Be Responsible for Completing the Evaluation and Reporting the Results. Once the previous step is determined, it will be very easy to specify who will be responsible for completing the evaluation and reporting the results. If the evaluation will be conducted internally, it is important to specify the person who will be responsible for this. Usually, the school principal or a district-level administrator is given the overall responsibility for completing the evaluation and reporting the results. At other times, specific teachers are assigned this task depending upon their interest, size, and scope of the project and the time required to complete the task.

The external evaluator is usually given the responsibility for completing the evaluation and reporting the results. It is absolutely essential that this person be in close contact with project participants, teachers, and administrators to keep lines of communication open and to develop credibility with the staff. It is not the role of the external evaluator to concentrate only on the negatives of the project, but rather to identify those areas that are being implemented successfully and to offer suggestions for refinement, revision, and improvement.

Utilizing the Evaluation Results for Program Refinement, Revision, and Improvement. Project participants, administrators, teachers, board members, and others should welcome an external evaluation of their program. Having the feedback of an outside resource person who is unbiased and offers suggestions for refinement, revision, and improvement is a good thing for your project and could help to ensure possible continuation funding for years two and three.

Once the results are in for the mid-year evaluation of your project, this gives the entire staff and administration time to make the needed changes to improve and refine program offerings, to acquire additional facilities, staff, and materials, if needed, and to do what it takes to get ready for the second half of the school year.

The end-of-year evaluation report provides the school district with information concerning the entire year's results, including suggestions for improvement. It also provides the funding agency with a report to assist the agency in deciding whether to extend the funding for another year and helps to determine if the money was well spent.

Assignment 4

Evaluation

1. Study the following Quality of Project Evaluation (5 points) section taken from the program review criteria of the "21st Century Community Learning Centers Program."

   Quality of Project Evaluation (5 points)

   The extent to which the methods of evaluation include the use of objective performance measures that are clearly related to the intended outcomes of the project and will produce quantitative and qualitative data to the extent possible.

   Go to Chapter 6 and review the evaluation section of the twenty-first Century Community Learning Centers Program on pages 109–114. In groups of three to five, discuss whether the application meets the quality review criteria above and give it a score of 1 through 5 points. Be prepared to defend your scoring of this section.
2. Utilizing the Mini-Grant Application on pages 71–73 write the evaluation component that corresponds to your activities and each program objective that you have written.
3. Number each section of the evaluation component to correspond to the numbering system for each objective.
4. In groups of three to five, distribute copies of your evaluation plan, analyze the evaluation component for each objective, and make suggestions for improvement.

The Project Budget

The budget that you present to the funding agency delineates the costs involved in carrying out your project and expresses what you are trying to accomplish. It is essential that you prepare this section with a great deal of care and competence because it has an impact on your credibility with the funding agency. People reading your project will look very carefully at the budget figures you present to see if they reflect the activities that you describe in your narrative statement and the overall scope of the project. If you ask for too much money or too little money, or if your budget figures are unrealistic, the reviewers will usually recognize it. Additionally, if your budget format is unfamiliar to the reviewer, it probably says that you either did not follow directions or lack the experience necessary to fully carry out the project. It behooves you to get help from your school principal, the district accountant, or the business manager as you put together the budget piece. These people can also assist you with specific figures for salaries, fringe benefits, consultants, hourly rates for noncertificated personnel, materials, equipment, indirect costs, and other matters. They can also help you in formatting the material so that it is clear and understandable.

When preparing a budget, answer the following questions. Does the budget:

■ Present a format that is consistent with the funding agency's requirements?

■ Relate to the objectives and activities of the project?

■ Provide the necessary resources to carry out the project?

■ Provide necessary detail so that the reviewer understands how specific budget categories were calculated?

■ Separate the indirect costs from the direct costs?

■ Include a budget narrative explaining how you arrived at specific budget calculations for each budget category?

Presenting a Budget Format That Is Consistent with the Funding Agency's Requirements

In writing a federal grant, the government asks you to complete U.S. Department of Education, Budget Information, Non-Construction Programs (ED Form No. 524). See Appendix 1 for copy of form, including Instructions for ED Form No. 524. In addition to completing the form, the government asks that you provide an itemized budget breakdown (line item budget) by project year for each budget category listed.

Budget Categories

1. Personnel
2. Fringe Benefits
3. Travel
4. Equipment
5. Supplies
6. Contractual
7. Construction
8. Other
9. Total Direct Costs (Lines 1–8)
10. Indirect Costs (see below)
11. Training Stipends
12. Total Costs (Lines 9–11)

The budget categories above provide you with a format that you can use with other funding agencies such as corporations and foundations, unless they have their own format for you to complete. Of course, only use those categories that apply to your project.

Each budget category presented should relate to the objectives and activities of the project. This should be obvious to the reviewer. Nothing in the budget should stand out as being irrelevant, too costly, or not needed. These are "red flags" that you do not want to raise.

Providing the Necessary Resources to Adequately Carry Out the Project

While you do not want to propose anything that would be irrelevant, too costly, or not needed, you also want to make certain that you have enough resources delineated in the budget to adequately carry out the project. I have seen funding agencies turn down projects that do not ask for enough money to meet the objectives of the project. I have also seen funding agencies increase program budgets when they like a project, score it high, and are convinced that the applicants did not ask for enough money. A funding agency might want you to beef up specific sections of the budget, suggest increasing salaries for particular positions, or request that you employ an external evaluator. If this be the case, they will usually ask you to resubmit a "revised budget."

Providing the necessary resources to adequately carry out the project is not a simple task. Asking for too much or too little money is not the way to go. Schedule time to do your homework, contact resource people both in the school district and outside the district, refer to this book as needed, and develop a budget request that is meaningful and meets the objectives and activities of your project head on.

Providing the Necessary Detail

When working on your itemized budget breakdown, sometimes referred to as a "Line Item Budget," provide the necessary detail to enable the reviewer to understand how specific budget categories were calculated. For example, if under "Travel" you have a budget figure of $3,000, indicate how that money will be spent—for example, one roundtrip to Washington, DC for two staff members @ $500 each, includes per diem. ASCD Conference in San Franciso for four staff members @ $125 each, includes per diem. **Note:** Further elaboration of each budget item will appear in the Budget Narrative section.

Separating the Direct Costs from the Indirect Costs

Calculating the Direct Costs   Direct costs are those costs in items 1 through 8 above that are specifically related to the proposed project such as personnel, fringe benefits, travel, supplies (materials), equipment, and contractural. Each of these categories have a number of subcategories. For example, under Personnel, break out both Certificated Personnel and Noncertificated Personnel. For Fringe Benefits, do the same. For Travel, breakout the number of trips, the locations, and the number of staff traveling. For Supplies, specify what you intend to buy and how much each of the items is going to cost. For Equipment, do the same. Under Contractural, list any consultants that you are planning to bring in, such as an External Evaluator at a daily rate—for example, External Evaluator, $4,000 (10 days @ $400 per day). **Note:** Most federal projects, corporations, and foundations do not provide monies for construction costs. They do provide funding at times for leasing office and classroom space. Check this out with your funding agency contact person. The Other category in the program application is a catch-all for all items that do not fit comfortably in the other categories. For example, you might want to include budget figures for postage, mail outs, publications, curriculum development, duplication costs, and others.

Calculating the Indirect Costs Indirect costs are often referred to as administrative or overhead costs. These costs are difficult to quantify and pin down. For example: The amount of time that the district accountant and other administrators spend on budgetary assistance such as payroll, accounting, and general project administration; the cost of utilities, custodial, and facilities; and the use of district-owned materials and equipment such as copiers and computers.

Indirect costs are usually figured as a percentage of the grant by the federal government. Contact your principal or district office administrator to find out if you have an assigned Indirect Cost Ratio for both federal and state grants. If not, using a 5 percent to 6 percent figure of the total grant request would be acceptable. Some corporate and foundation funding agencies allow you to use an Indirect Cost Ratio and some do not. Make certain that it is permissible to use this before inserting it into a corporate or foundation grant request.

How to Write a Budget Narrative

Whether it is required or not, it is a good idea to include a budget narrative explaining how you arrived at specific calculations for each budget category. This is usually accomplished through a narrative statement in paragraph form breaking down each budget category. If you do your homework, gather the needed data, talk to the right people, and get help as needed, the budget narrative should not be difficult to complete.

See Line Item Budget and Budget Narrative for successful "21st Century Community Learning Centers Program" on pages 116–121.

Assignment 5

Budgets

1. Develop a line item budget for the project that you have written objectives and activities for, using the 12 budget categories listed in the sample mini-grant application on pages 71–73.
2. Make copies and distribute your line item budget to a critique group of three to five persons.
3. Critique each other's line item budget and make suggestions for improvement.

How to Write a Dissemination Plan

Some funding agencies ask you to include a dissemination section in your application telling how you plan to let others know about your accomplishments at the conclusion of the project year. Preparing a comprehensive dissemination plan will help generate positive publicity and recognition for your project and for the funding agency. Some approaches you can use to disseminate information about your project both locally and nationally are:

■ Submitting press releases to local and national newspapers

■ Appearing on local and national radio and television shows

■ Providing information on the school district website

■ Writing and distributing newsletters about the project

■ Writing articles for publication in relevant educational journals

■ Publishing a pamphlet or book about the project

■ Speaking at local, state, and national conferences and conventions

■ Speaking at local and national service organization meetings

■ Visiting other school districts and reporting results

■ Serving as a consultant to other school districts

■ Conducting workshops and seminars at colleges and universities

I have found that providing a dissemination plan for your grant proposal (whether requested or not) will increase your chances of getting funded. Prepare the dissemination plan in paragraph form using some of the ideas above, and add additional ideas that are relevant.

How to Write the Program Summary and Abstract

Most federal grant applications and some corporate and foundation grant applications require a one-page program summary and abstract. The abstract should briefly describe the needs being addressed in the project, including the numbers and types of participants to be served, the objectives and activities proposed to meet them, the intended outcomes, and the budget request. Because the reviewer will read this piece first, extreme care should be taken to carefully summarize the project in a clear and concise manner. Make certain that it is well done, truly reflects the essence of your project, and creates an immediate favorable impression. It is recommended that this section be written last since you will have a clearer understanding of your total project at that time.

Some Helpful Hints to Improve Your Chances of Getting Funded

- Plan your writing schedule so that you have enough time to complete the task, gather signatures and approvals, and meet the deadline.

- Do not send your project in early because the more time you have with it, the more time you have to edit, revise, rewrite, reduce, and rearrange.

- Make certain that you follow the exact guidelines of the funding agency. Go over the guidelines on a continuing basis to be sure that you are not leaving anything out.

- Comply with the funding agency's instructions to use a specific type style and type size such as Times Roman, 12 pt, with double spacing and a maximum of 20 pages for the narrative. Give it to the funding agency exactly the way it has been described. If not specified, it is still a good idea to use a type style and type size that is clear, understandable, and double spaced.

- Use lists and tables. They convey a lot of information in a small amount of space. They are also easy to read and present a welcome change for the reviewer.

- Use bold type instead of underlining to emphasize key points or sections of the application. Be careful not to overuse, because it can be distracting to the reviewer.

- Use the same headings and subheadings in your application as the reviewers use in the evaluation form. Request a copy of the reviewers' evaluation form from the program officer for your project. If the form is not available, follow the application format exactly the way it is presented, and use the same headings and subheadings that appear in the application.

- When putting your application together, include just the essentials in the appendices. Check the program guidelines for any special requirements. Government grant applications sometimes ask that you place the following into the appendices: letters of support, letters of commitment, the names of consortium members, resumes, job descriptions, and organizational charts.

- Use a ragged right margin rather than a justified right margin because it is easier to read.

- Number your pages consecutively in the top right or center bottom of the each page.

- Prepare a table of contents that corresponds to your headings and subheadings.

- Before submitting your proposal, proofread it over and over again. Have several other people proofread it as well. Look for any typographical errors, misspellings, and mistakes in punctuation, grammar, facts, figures, charts, graphs, phone numbers, web addresses, and budget computations. Study the content carefully to make certain that it conveys what you are trying to say. Make changes as needed.

■ Make certain that you have made arrangements for duplication and collation of your application, allowing you enough time to make your final check of the application to see that pages are collated properly and that nothing is left out or misplaced in the application. If time is available, this is also a good time to make extra copies of the application for your needs. Otherwise, keep at least one hard copy for yourself and save the manuscript on the hard drive of your computer.

■ Deliver the completed application to the post office or another carrier in plenty of time to meet the deadline.

After You Receive the Grant, Then What?

When you are notified of a grant award and have received the money, you have good reason to be elated. You also have an opportunity to enhance the image of your school district by announcing the grant to the world. First, make certain that the funding agency agrees to allow you to make the announcement of the grant award. After you get the go ahead, put together some press releases for the local newspapers and other media and announce the grant on the district or school website. Second, take every opportunity to talk about the grant at conferences, workshops, and to organizations like the PTA, Kiwanis, and Rotary. It is enlightening to discover that once you start receiving grants and gifts, you begin developing a reputation for having quality programs. This in turn alerts other funding agencies about your school or school district and makes it easier for your school to get additional funding. People who know this phenomenon write grants and apply for monies on a continuing basis. This is how the rich get richer in education when it comes to writing grants.

As the project begins to be implemented, it is very important that you carry out your responsibilities in a professional manner and be good stewards of the money. This implies setting up sound accounting practices for the actual expenditure of the funds. In many school districts the accounting department or business office is assigned the responsibility to do the bookkeeping for external grants or gifts. In other school districts, the individual school site principals are responsible to keep track of grants and gifts for their sites. As mentioned elsewhere, many funding agencies, including the federal government, allow you to use an Indirect Cost Ratio to help defray some of the extra accounting and administrative costs brought on by the grant. The amount, usually about 5 percent to 7 percent of the total grant, should be included when submitting your overall budget proposal. It would be difficult to negotiate an Indirect Cost Ratio after the grant is approved.

Keeping in touch with your program officer is vitally important. Each approved project usually has a program officer (or someone else with a similar title) assigned to the project. Communicate with this person on a continuing basis. Let the program officer know how the project is progressing and invite this person to visit your project along with other members of the staff. Be open and honest in your communication with the program officer and talk about the problems as well as the successes you are having. Ask for assistance when you need it. Program officers know that everything is not going to run smoothly at first. They would rather you be honest with them than cover up any problems you are having.

The site principal is generally considered the instructional leader of the school. The principal is also one of the key players in the implementation of a successful project or program. Without the total support of the principal, your project will probably not succeed. Seek out the support of the principal and include this person in your planning, deliberations, and program evaluation. Develop a good relationship with the external evaluator. Communicate with this person both formally and informally during the implementation of the project. Ask for input and suggestions for improvement related to the overall progress of the project.

Communicate and ask for input from program participants, be they students, parents, teachers, staff, or others. Make certain that the participants play a major role in the evaluation of the overall program. Provide staff training and in-service as described in your program proposal. If you have indicated in your proposal that you will have a project advisory group made up of community members, parents, teachers, and others that meets monthly, make certain that this takes place. It is critical that the services you promised in the program proposal are carried out. Continue to assess your needs as the project progresses and study the possibility of continuation funding for years two and three.

Extra Assignment

Begin to Write Your Own Federal Grant Application

1. Start thinking about a project that you would like to work on that the federal government might be interested in funding.
2. Begin to do prospect research on the internet about available funding opportunities in this area.
3. Request a hard copy of the application or download it from your computer and study it very carefully.
4. Search various websites to gather research data in your area of interest and be prepared to quote experts in your area of interest.
5. Develop a filing system for your materials.
6. Gather needs assessment documentation for your project.
7. Write goals, objectives, activities, and evaluation specifications for your project.
8. Put together the budget and the budget justification for the project.
9. Write a dissemination plan for the project.
10. Write a one-page summary of your project and distribute it to the class.
11. Be prepared to discuss project with class.

Mini-Grant Program Application

Your Name _____ Date _____

School or School District _____

Address _____

e-mail _____ Telephone _____

1.0 Title of Project _____
_____

2.0 Summary of the Project (50 words or less) _____
_____
_____
_____

3.0 Needs Assessment Documentation _____
_____
_____
_____
_____
_____
_____
_____
_____
_____
_____

NOTES: Present both hard and soft data. Cite research findings, if available, to justify why the problem should be investigated.

3.0 OVERALL GOAL OF THE PROJECT _____
_____
_____

4.0 OBJECTIVES OF THE PROJECT (Write four measurable objectives)

4.1 _____
_____

4.2 _____
_____

4.3 _____
_____

4.4 _____
_____

(continued)

Mini-Grant Program Application (continued)

5.0 ACTIVITIES (Write at least two activities for each objective)

5.1 _____

_____

_____

5.2 _____

_____

_____

5.3 _____

_____

_____

5.4 _____

_____

_____

6.0 EVALUATION SPECIFICATIONS (Describe how you will evaluate each objective)

6.1 _____

_____

_____

6.2 _____

_____

_____

6.3 _____

_____

_____

6.4 _____

_____

7.0 ESTIMATED BUDGET (By Category)

7.1 Personnel   _____

7.2 Fringe Benefits   _____

7.3 Travel   _____

7.4 Equipment   _____

7.5 Supplies and Materials _____

7.6 Contractural   _____

7.7 Construction   _____

7.8 Other   _____

7.9 TOTAL DIRECT COSTS   _____
(Lines 7.1-7.8)

7.10 INDIRECT COSTS   _____
(Use 6%)

7.11 Training Stipends   _____

7.12 TOTAL COSTS   _____
(Lines 7.9-7.11)

8.0 BUDGET JUSTIFICATION (Briefly justify the above budget figures and elaborate on any budgetary category that needs further elaboration.)

_____
_____
_____
_____
_____
_____
_____
_____

9.0 WHY SHOULD THIS GRANT APPLICATION BE FUNDED? (In 50 words or less, justify why you think this grant application should be funded.)

_____
_____
_____
_____

BIBLIOGRAPHY

Grantwriting

1. Carlson, Mim. *Winning Grants Step by Step: Support Centers of America's Complete Workbook for Planning, Developing and Writing Successful Proposals.* Jossey-Bass Publishers, San Francisco, CA.
2. Ferguson, Jacqueline. *Grants for Schools: How to Find and Win Funds for K-12 Programs* (3rd ed.). Capitol Publications, Alexandria, VA.
3. Gooch, Judith Mirick. *Writing Winning Proposals.* Council for Advancement and Support of Education. Washington, DC.
4. Hale, Phale. *Writing Grant Proposals that Win.* Capitol Publications, Alexandria, VA.

5. Miner, Lynn E., Jeremy T. Miner, & Jerry Griffith. *Proposal Planning and Writing* (2nd ed.). Oryx Press, Phoenix, AZ.

Internet Resources

1. *Developing and Writing Grant Proposals.* Catalog of Federal Domestic Assistance.
    Web Access: *http://www.cfda.gov/public/cat-writing.htm*
2. *EPA Grantwriting Tutorial.* Environmental Protection Agency.
    Web Access: *http://www.epa.gov/seahome/grants.html*
3. Miner, Jeremy T., & Lynn E. Miner. *Guide to Proposal Planning and Writing.* Oryx Press.
    Web Access: *http://www.oryxpress.com/miner.htm*
4. *Proposal Writing Short Course.* The Foundation Center, New York.
    Web Access: *http://fdncenter.org/onlib/shortcourse/prop1.html*
5. *Writing a Winning Grant Proposal.* Grant Writing in South Washington County Schools, Cottage Grove, MN.
    Web Access: *http://www.sowashco.k12.mn.us/grants/Handbook/writing.htm*

Evaluation

1. Gray, Sandra Trice. *Evaluation with Power: A New Approach to Organizational Effectiveness, Empowerment, and Excellence.* Jossey-Bass Publishers, San Francisco, CA.
2. Van Mannan, John. *The Process of Program Evaluation.* The Grantmanship Center, Los Angeles, CA.
3. Wholey, Joseph, Harry P. Hatry, & Kathryn E. Newcomer, (Eds.). *Handbook of Practical Program Evaluation.* Jossey-Bass Publishers, San Francisco, CA.

6

Samples of Successful Mini-Grants and Corporate and Foundation Grants

In this chapter you will:

❒ Study winning grant applications including mini-grants and corporate and foundation grants

❒ Identify different writing styles, formatting, and winning strategies

❒ Identify the different requirements of the various funding agencies

❒ Discover individual differences among applications

Following are some samples of successful grant applications. All of these applications have been funded. By reading and studying this chapter, you will gain valuable experience and insight into how projects are written, grant application formatting, writing styles, and requirements of various funding agencies. Listed below are the names of the grant writers, their affiliations, and the names of the funding agencies.

1. Application to the San Diego Foundation Teacher's Fund, Project Writer—Robert S. Greenamyer, Park Village Elementary School, Poway Unified School District, Poway, California.

2. Application to the South Washington Education Foundation, Project Writer—Sharon Miller Thompson with the help and advice of others, Park High School, South Washington County Schools, Cottage Grove, Minnesota.

3. Application to the Alliance Healthcare Foundation, Project Writer—Stanley Levenson with the help and advice of others, National School District, National City, California.

Application Submitted to the San Diego Foundation Teacher's Fund: "Pictures to Create Thousands of Words"

I. Project Description

1. Having a video camera system and flatbed scanner in my classroom will enhance the continuance of two projects that I have developed over the past two years. The first project, **P-3 News,** is a weekly classroom broadcast of world, national, state, local, and school news, sports, entertainment, and weather. Throughout the week, students work as a table team to prepare for their Friday newscast. They gather the news, get interviews ready, write their script, and rehearse before we "shoot." Currently, we borrow the school video camera and tripod to do our taping. In a school of 1,000, this can be a trick! Having our own **video camera system** in our class will ease the preparation of the weekly show. Having a more portable video camera will allow us to shoot "on location" occasionally.

My secondary project involves student-created PowerPoint presentations. Last year, student cooperative groups created presentations on Colonial America, highlighting food, jobs, clothing, schooling, and customs in 10- to 20-slide presentations. They were taught PowerPoint and then researched their colonial region to develop their show. Students wrote a presentation plan prior to using PowerPoint for their final product. Pictures for this project were scanned from a central flatbed scanner to our school network. The scanner is located in another building across campus (I'm out in a portable building). Having a **flatbed scanner and high-quality graphics software** in our classroom will allow students immediate access to the materials they need to scan photos and create their presentations.

2. Both of these interdisciplinary projects address learning skills in writing, reading, social studies, planning, and cooperation. The projects simulate real-world situations where people gather information and synthesize it into a presentation or product. The challenging projects have been highly motivating to my students, generating lots of expository writing and research.

3. This project is ongoing and occurs weekly in my classroom throughout the year.

II. Demographic and Student Profile

1. All students in my fifth grade class of 28 will participate in these projects. I have an upper-middle class, multiethnic, heterogeneous class that includes gifted students, resource students, and a range in between. All my students are 10 to 11 years old.

III. Learning Objectives

1. The specific learning objectives of this project are to:

*   increase expository writing skills by writing news scripts and research reports

- increase knowledge of the world by reading the newspaper for relevant news
- increase reading for information skills by reading the newspaper and relevant history books or articles
- synthesize gathered materials into a coherent presentation
- work cooperatively as a team with other students to accomplish a high level task

2. This project will increase my teaching effectiveness by using time and equipment more efficiently and providing a motivating focus for student learning. I will learn more about communication technology and will share this with my students. I will no longer have to spend valuable time tracking down equipment for use in these projects.

3. As noted in my project description and learning objectives, *P-3 News* and student Colonial America presentations have been highly motivating learning activities. Social studies and current events can be a dry subject; incorporating technology and becoming researchers and presenters have brought history and current events to life for my students. In the age of information and communication, this project addresses both these areas for my students.

4. As noted in the objectives above, students will learn to write, read, research a topic, synthesize information, and cooperate with others to create a product.

IV. Sharing Your Ideas

1. This project will be easily replicated and sustained beyond the grant since the materials requested will last for many years beyond the grant year.

2. I have shared *P-3 News* and PowerPoint presentation projects with my teaching partners. I will continue to do so.

V. Evaluation

1. The benefit of project-based learning is that there is a project at the end. *P-3 News* and PowerPoint presentations will be evaluated for quality writing and research. Scripts will be assessed and cooperation will be monitored.

VI. Budget

1. The per pupil cost of this project is estimated to be: $960/150 students = $6.50

2. I anticipate the video camera system, flatbed scanner, and graphic software will last at least 5 years (hence, 150 students, 5×30 in #1 above; probably more)

3. This project will support *P-3 News* and other school or class events, as well as PowerPoint presentations in social studies and science. The itemized budget is

• Sony video camera, tapes, charger	$500
• tripod, bag	$ 60
• HP Scanjet flatbed scanner	$250
• Adobe Photo Shop graphics software	$150
(estimated tax included)	
Total amount request =	**$960**

Application Submitted to the to the South Washington County Education Foundation

South Washington County Education Foundation Educator Initiative Program Application

Name of Applicants:

Name of Project Contact Person:

School: Park High School

Grades: 10–12

Project Title: Park Pride 2000, Wolfpack Sculpture Garden

Project Description:
Park High School students in art (ceramics), industrial technology (metals), and biology (horticulture) will work collaboratively to design, and install a Wolfpack 2000 Sculpture Garden. The sculpture garden is based on Park's mascot, the Wolfpack. It will be installed in a garden setting at the main entrance of Park High. The sculpture garden project will provide opportunities for students to master and demonstrate skills and strategies using an interdisciplinary, cooperative, and authentic learning model.

Program Goal:
To implement a project-based interdisciplinary education program giving students the opportunity to work collaboratively to design, analyze, and problem solve. The project will develop knowledge and skills and increase the participating students' pride and sense of ownership at Park High School.

Rationale:
Current research shows that experiential learning related to authentic, real-life situations is more valuable to the learner. Given these learning opportunities, lessons integrate with prior knowledge more thoroughly and become more deeply imbedded in the learners' knowledge base. Businesses tell us that students need to be able to work cooperatively, analyze situations, and solve problems relating to complex data in the world of work. Based on these premises, the Park Pride 2000 project becomes an opportunity for groups of students from three disciplines to gain new strategies for success after high school. The authentic learning experiences set in cooperative learning style will engage students who each bring diverse skills and valuable prior knowledge bases to the project while building long lasting skills and attitudes for success. All students will need to learn from each other and solve problems with variables both inside and outside their own knowledge base.

Students will draft and design in 2-D form and implement ideas in 3-D forms, following through to completion of finished project. Ceramics students will research, create a theme, design to scale, and produce terra cotta murals centering on the Wolfpack. Metals students will research, analyze, and correlate stress factors and produce ten 10" tall kiosks. Horticulture students will research and assess area soil conditions, analyze various plant types for size, visual characteristics, care needs, and climate. They will design and implement the design using this data and limitations presented by the sculptures. The Park Pride 2000 project helps the District meet the Minnesota Graduation Standards by developing skills in 9 of the 10 learning areas. The learning areas include: 1) read, view, listen; 2) write and speak; 3) literature and the arts: 4) math applications; 5) inquiry; 6) scientific applications; 7) people and cultures; 8) decision making; and 9) resource management. The project also helps advance the 1999–2000 school board goals. The project is directly applicable to goal #4 to provide opportunities for all students to be more successful with an emphasis on career development.

Outcomes:

1. Ceramics, metals, and horticulture students will demonstrate skills mastery in respective disciplines based on average to above average scores on a skill checklist completed by teacher(s) through project observation.
2. 100 percent of all students participants will be able to identify at least 5 individual strengths and 2 weakness areas while working on a team.
3. 85 percent of all students will demonstrate the ability to research, analyze, and integrate information and ideas into project implementation based upon a project skill checklist completed by teachers and analysis of the students' diaries/reflection assignments.

Description of Instructional Procedures, Approaches, Methods, or Activities:

* Teachers will act as facilitators—coordinating student discussions, prioritizing work, and setting schedules.
* Cooperative learning modules will be set within and between subject areas, relating to design and creation.
* Cross-teacher-driven activities and updates relating to construction progress and issues
* Problem solving group meetings relating to individual vs. group issues and other project difficulties
* Teacher-driven skill review and skill building activities needed to accomplish given tasks.
* Student-created checklists, task lists, and rubrics shared in small, large, and interdisciplinary groups.
* Students view the video/still documentary story of the building of the sculpture garden prior to writing the final reflective growth summary.

Evaluation Procedures:

Program success is defined as meeting all 3 objectives outlined in the Outcomes section. The project manager will be responsible for overseeing evaluation procedures. A final report will be created and disseminated to team members and the Education Foundation.

* **Observation:** Students will be observed working in ceramics, metals, and horticulture by teachers to evaluate skill and knowledge levels. Teachers will use the skill checklist with a rating scale of needs improvement, average, and above average.
* **Student journals/papers:** Students will be required to complete the following: Write a pre-project personal intent statement covering their vision and role on the project; reflect on the process of designing

through large group activities in written summary form; write a mid-point statement regarding progress, experiences, project vision, and suggestions for project improvements; write a post-project statement on personal contributions and ideas for program improvement; and write a final reflective growth summary, including a comparison of this project with other classroom experience.

- **Program improvements:** Two roundtable Next Steps discussions will be facilitated by teachers throughout the project period. Additionally, teachers will review midpoint student papers including a section on suggestions for program improvements. Continuous improvements in the process will be implemented based on staff discussion, student feedback, and journal suggestions.

Identify Any School or Community Partners Involved in the Project and Their Roles:

- Park's art, industrial technology, and biology departments—interdisciplinary creation of curriculum modules to create Park Pride 2000.
- Park administration—gap funding for creation of the sculpture garden. Providing outdoor lighting system once garden is completed.
- Bailey's Nursery—request $75 for plant material and $200—Target—for disposable cameras/video.
- Famous Dave's Ribs/Quizno's Subs—request dinners for winter and fall Next Steps discussions.
- Heritage Bank and Burnet Realty—request $200 for student recognition plaques

PROJECT TIMELINE

Date	Activity	Party Responsible
Sept. 1999	Teachers meet to integrate tasks and skills building lesson into curriculum	Project Mgr/teachers
Sept. 1999	Materials for kiosks and mural tiles ordered	Teachers
Sept. 1999	Students meet to prioritize needs and create overall design	Project Manager
Oct. 1999	Students begin creating mural tiles and creating jigs for kiosks	Teachers
Oct. 1999	Next Steps dinner and student roundtable	Project Manager
Mid Nov. 1999	First kiosk goes together, process critique & reflection	Teachers
Dec. 1999	Work on mural tiles and kiosks continues, horticulture students begin plans and plant research	Project Manager & Horticulture
Jan. 2000	Next Steps dinner and student roundtable discussions	Project Manager
Feb. 2000	Plants order	Horticulture
Apr. 2000	Kiosks completed and installed, garden made ready & planted	Project Manager/Hort.
May 2000	Wolfpack Sculpture Garden unveiled	Project Manager/ teachers
May 2000	Completion and student recognition celebration	Project Manager/ teachers

Detailed Project Budget

Expense Item	Foundation	Park HS	Private Donations	Total
Equipment				
Slab Roller		$ 760.50		$ 760.50
Disposable Cameras & Videotape			200.00	200.00
Materials				
Clay	300.00		200.00	500.00
Aluminum	2,700.00	1,795.00		4,495.00
Anodizing		1,000.00		1,000.00
Copper		150.00	100.00	250.00
Plants		150.00	75.00	175.00
Site Preparation				
Demolition		300.00		300.00
Footings		500.00		500.00
Lighting Systems		1,000.00		1,000.00
Instructional Expenses				
Printing/Copying		75.00		75.00
Student Recognition				
Dinners, awards, and plaques			1,030.00	1,030.00
Total by Group	3,000.00	5,730.50	1,605.00	10,335.50

Application Submitted to the Alliance Healthcare Foundation

Proposal to the Alliance Healthcare Foundation for the Inclusion of a Healthcare Component for the Parents as Teachers Program

DESCRIPTION OF HEALTH PROBLEM AND A STATEMENT OF NEED

The National School District, located in San Diego county, 12 miles north of the United States border with Mexico, in National City, California, encompasses preschool through grade six in ten schools, serving approximately 6,331 students. More than 90% of the students are from minority groups, and more than 70% are Hispanic. With an ethically diverse population of 54,000 and an average income that is less than half the national average, National City ranks as the 13th poorest urbanized area in America. The median income for National City in 1995 was $19,562 adjusted for inflation. This is the lowest median income for all jurisdictions in the State of California.

In 1993, a comprehensive needs assessment was conducted by the National City Collaborative to help identify the health and social service needs of National City residents and identify service inconsistencies. A broad-based participation survey was utilized that included input from parents, community members, agency workers, and educators and included the following:

a. Sixty families, representing the City's ethnic and socioeconomic diversity, responded to intensive, one-on-one, in-depth interviews. These families were self-selected from a pool of 50% Chapter I (Compensatory Education) families, 20% LEP (Limited English Proficient) families, and 30% from other families identified by the school sites, the probation department and community agencies. The ethnic breakdown for the families interviewed was as follows: Hispanic (75%); White (18%); African American (7%); Native American (4%); Filipino (2%).

b. After key areas of need were identified by the 60 families, more than 70 community members participated in open forums, which were held at two school sites to assist in prioritizing and expanding the identified needs.

c. Personnel from 38 health, education, and social agencies also provide input on community needs and barriers to existing services.

d. Focus groups were organized in six different categories including public agencies, elementary and secondary schools, law enforcements and emergency services, health and mental health agencies, and community service organizations.

e. A collaborative work group studied the demographics of the community and also looked closely at services available to National City residents.

THREE MAJOR AREAS OF NEED WERE IDENTIFIED BY THE 1993 SURVEY AND THE WORK OF THE FOCUS GROUPS:

1. Access to and information regarding health services
2. Access to and information regarding social services
3. Strengthening partnerships and relationships between the parents, the community and the schools in regard to addressing identified needs.

ORGANIZATION OF THE NATIONAL CITY COLLABORATIVE AND THE FAMILY RESOURCE CENTER AT KIMBALL SCHOOL

In an attempt to meet the needs described above, the National City Collaborative was formed in 1993, as part of a larger statewide and national approach to utilizing multi-institutional collaboration to make services more responsive to child and family needs. Spearheaded by the County Department of Social Services and supported by a Department of Health and Human Services grant as well as grants from the State of California Healthy Start Program and the State AB 1741 Blended Funding Pilot grant, more than 20 public and private organizations joined together with community members to inaugurate a Family Resource Center (FRC) in 1995 at Kimball Elementary School. At the FRC, parents, volunteers, social workers, and healthcare providers join together in supporting families as primary caregivers, generating greater self-sufficiency and parent involvement of families. Some of the services offered include immunizations for babies and children, health screening, job referrals, and employment training. The majority of program activities are being supported by redirected and in-kind contributions.

INCLUSION OF THE PAT PROGRAM INTO THE FRC

As the implementation of the Family Resource Center began to take place, a need existed for the services of a PAT Educator. in that the National School District has been considered one of the "leaders" in the nation as related to the PAT Program and is also the West Coast Training Site, the FRC requested and received from the district the services of a part-time (20 hours per week) PAT Educator as an in-kind contribution to the project. The virtual success of the PAT Educator in working with the parents as true partners, has lead to the employment of five part-time community members who were hired for a Home Support Apprenticeship. These new staff were trained as PAT Educators and have taken a leadership role in engaging the community and organizing activities for the resource center.

While good progress has been made by the PAT Educators, as of February 1997, access to low-cost, basic, preventive healthcare information regarding health and social services, language and cultural barriers, and access to adult educational opportunities still remain the prevalent unaddressed needs identified by families, community groups, school administrators, teachers, and others.

AN OPPORTUNITY TO BRING ABOUT CHANGE

The National School District affiliated with the National Parents as Teachers (PAT) Program in St. Louis, Missouri, in 1987 for the purpose of involving the parents in the school district as "true partners" in the education of their children. The PAT Program is based on the concept that parents are their child's first and most influential teachers and that experiences in the beginning years of a child's life are critical in laying the foundation for later success in school, at work and as a parent. Parents as Teachers offers families regularly scheduled personal home visits by certified bilingual home support educators who provide timely information on the child's development and suggest practical ways to encourage learning. Group meetings are held where parents can share their experiences and common concerns and gain new insights. Periodic monitoring and formal screening of children's development for early detection of learning handicaps or developmental delays take place on a continuing basis.

The nationally recognized Parents as Teachers Curriculum includes specific, age-related lesson plans and developmentally appropriate handouts for parents of 0- to 5-year-old children. While some provisions have been made for health education by PAT, no curriculum material have been produced that address major health issues and health needs.

THE PROJECT OBJECTIVES

The National School District, working cooperatively with the National City Collaborative, proposes the following objectives to meet the health needs of at least 125 families of 0- to 5-year-old children in the district:

1.   To develop a comprehensive Health Education Component, including age-appropriate curriculum materials for the Parents as Teachers Program in the summer of 1997, to be used with parent participants of 0- to 5-year-old children in the National School District during the 1997–98 academic year.

2.   To provide staff training for all the Home Support Educators in the summer of 1997 and at least once a month during the school year in the utilization and implementation of the Health Education Component.

3.   To employ a recognized consultant in the summer of 1997 and into 1997–98 school year to work cooperatively with the parents and the staff in providing the necessary leadership in the development of the curriculum materials and in the staff development program.

4.   To show significant "pre" to "post" test gains for parents of 0- to 5-year-old children related to understanding of health services, social services, immunizations, dental care, eye care, safety issues, substance abuse, nutrition, and personal wellness.

5.   To disseminate the results of the program throughout San Diego County, the State of California, and the United States.

The following activities will be implemented to meet the needs of the project:

DETAILED DESCRIPTION OF THE PROJECT

ACTIVITIES TO MEET THE NEEDS OF THE PROJECT	TIMETABLE
1. A Curriculum Development Advisory Group (CDAG) will be formed for the purpose of providing input to the National School District and the National City Collaborative in carrying out the project and in the development of the curriculum materials. Parents, healthcare professionals, and staff will be called upon to assist in the development of the curriculum and to serve as resource personnel to the school district and to the Home Support Educators.	May 15, 1997– June 30, 1998
2. A Health Education Consultant will be employed to provide the necessary leadership and direction for the project as related to curriculum development and staff development.	June 1, 1997
3. Curriculum materials will be developed in the summer, 1997 and field-tested during the 1997-98 school year. The curriculum will be built and integrated with new and existing health education materials, guidelines, and frameworks available through the State Department of	June 15, 1997– June 30, 1998

Education, the County Office of Education, libraries, hospitals, the World Wide Web and other resources. The use of technology will be incorporated as appropriate including a resource list of local providers of health-related services for utilization in the program.

4. Provide curriculum material and staff development for Home Support Educators in the following areas: accessing information regarding health services and social services; immunizations; dental care; eye care, safety issues; substance abuse; nutrition; personal wellness; and others.	June 15, 1997– June 30, 1998
5. Home Support Educators conduct home visitations and monthly large-group meetings throughout the 1997–98 school year to field-test new health education curriculum materials and articulate them with the PAT Program Activities.	Sept. 1, 1997– June 30, 1998
6. Conduct an Internal Evaluation for self-assessment purposes. Employ the services of an External Evaluator to do a comprehensive external evaluation including a written interim and final evaluation report to be made available to the funding agency, the school district, and others.	Sept. 1, 1997– June 30, 1998
7. Disseminate the results of the program throughout San Diego County, to the funding agency, to the State of California and throughout the United States, including the National Parents as Teachers Program. Administrators, key staff, parents, and other will make presentations and conduct workshops and meetings about the program. Press releases and professional articles will be published telling about the progress and successes of the program. Continue the program into the 1998–99 school year.	June 30, 1998– Sept. 1, 1998

EVALUATION PLAN

Both an internal and an external evaluation will take place. The internal evaluation will focus on self-improvement and include all staff involved in the project. It will provide opportunities to assess progress and change in ways that lead to greater achievement of the objectives of the project. The information gathered in the internal evaluation will be shared internally to assist in making individual and collective decisions that move the National School District and the children and parents it serves to new levels of excellence.

The external evaluation will be conducted by an External Evaluator who will have experience in health education, evaluation design, and program implementation. The External Evaluator will assist in locating relevant evaluation instrumentation and/or designing needed instrumentation. "Pre" and "post" tests (surveys) will be administered to the parents to determine the extent of understanding of health services and social services available to them. In addition, the External Evaluator will assess to what extent the objectives of the project were met and offer suggestions for improvement. Both an Interim Evaluation Report and a Final Evaluation Report will be provided by the External Evaluator. The results of the Evaluation Reports will assist in refining and improving the project.

STAFFING NEEDS OF THE PROJECT

1. 100 days of consultant time for professional staff to assist in the development of curriculum materials and conduct the staff development program.
2. Five part-time Home Support Staff to conduct home visits in the National City Community and to field-test new curriculum materials.
3. One full-time Nurse Practitioner for the purposes of providing nursing care and screenings as needed.
4. One part-time (25%) family counselor for counseling as needed.

OTHER NEEDS

1. Staff development, conferences, travel, mileage, supplies, books, materials, and software to supplement and enhance the program.
2. Printing, copying, telephone, fax, and indirect costs to administer the project.

BENEFITS DERIVED FROM THE PROJECT

1. Provides a much-needed health component to enhance the National City Parents as Teachers (PAT) Program
2. Has the potential for national exposure, recognition, adoption, and dissemination
3. Extends depth of contact between Home Support Staff and families to include health issues
4. Employs and trains local community members as parent educators
5. Teaches and reinforces prevention methods in healthcare
6. Provides access to professional health services at point of contact
7. Creates a health education curriculum to help teach parents how to maintain a healthy family on a one-to-one basis
8. Provides invaluable knowledge for families to internalize and take with them (beyond the PAT Program)
9. Articulates and extends the program into Head Start, preschool, and grades K–8
10. Takes advantage of current PAT Program that already exists in the homes and extends program to include health-related issues and services

NATIONAL SCHOOL DISTRICT
ALLIANCE HEALTHCARE FOUNDATION GRANT

APPROVED BUDGET (6-1-97)
1997–98

ITEM	AMOUNT APPROVED	DISTRICT CONTRIBUTION
Salaries and Wages		
Parents Educator/Coord. (100%)		$24,490
Director of Special Programs (10%)		7,000
Home Support Educators		
(5 @ 3.5 hrs.		
× 210 days × $10.07)	$37,007	
Nurse Practitioner (100%)	50,000	
Family Counselor (25%)	13,000	
Staff Development Training		12,500
Fringe Benefits and Payroll Taxes	25,002	16,670
Consultants and Professional Fees		
Development of Curriculum		
Materials and Staff Develop.		
(80 days @$300)	24,000	
External Evaluator		
(10 days @ $300)	3,000	
Travel, Conferences, Mileage	5,000	2,500
Supplies, Books, Materials,		
Software & Translation Services	6,000	7,500
Printing and Copying	3,500	4,500
Telephone and Fax	3,000	4,000
Postage and Delivery	2,500	3,500
Rent, Facilities, and Utilities		16,500
Indirect Costs (6.25%)	8,126	
	———	———
TOTALS	$180,135	$99,160

BUDGET NARRATIVE

The National School District has presented a budget request that is reasonable and is based upon the needs of the school district and the community we serve. The District will also be making a considerable contribution to the program through in-kind contributions totaling more than $99,000. The total amount requested from the Alliance Healthcare Foundation for this project is $180,135.

Under Salary and Wages, we are requesting that the Alliance Healthcare Foundation assist us with moneys for the employment of five part-time Home Support Educators who will be responsible for the delivery of services to the parents. These 3.5-hour positions do not require fringe benefits but are "key positions" in the project. Another "key position" in the project is a Health Education Consultant who will be employed as an independent contractor for 80 days for the purpose of coordinating the development of the curriculum materials and in providing for the staff development program. Additionally, we are requesting moneys for the employment of a part-time (25%) Family Counselor who will be providing family counseling services on a referral basis from the Home Support Educators as needed. An External Evaluation Consultant will be employed for ten days. The consultant will have experience in both health education and in the evaluation process.

To enable the staff to keep up with new trends in parent education and health education, and to encourage the staff to engage in professional activities, including speaking engagements that disseminate information about the project in California and elsewhere, we are requesting moneys for travel and conferences. In addition, some of the budget will also be used for mileage for the Home Support Educators who will be driving to the homes of the parents. In the Supplies, Books, Materials, and Software category we are in need of moneys for up-to-date cutting-edge supplies, books, and materials, including computer software and CD-ROMs. Finally, moneys are requested for "housekeeping" to include printing and copying, telephone and fax, postage and delivery, and indirect costs.

It should be noted that the National School District will be making a major financial commitment to the project by paying 100% for the Parent Educator/Trainer (including fringe benefits), providing for administrative oversight of the project by the Director of Special Program, and contributing (in-kind) $12,500 to staff development training. Additionally, the district will be contributing a total of $22,000 for travel, conferences, mileage, supplies, books, materials, computer software, and "housekeeping" necessities, and $16,500 in-kind for facilities and utilities.

The Nurse Practitioner position (100%) has been inserted into the budget with the approval of the Alliance Healthcare Foundation. This position is needed to fully carry out the project.

7

Sample of a Successful Federal Grant Application

In this chapter you will:

- ❐ Study a winning 21st Century Community Learning Centers Program Application

- ❐ Identify the application requirements and administrative regulations

- ❐ Discover the differences between this federal grant application and the mini-grants and foundation grant presented in Chapter 6

- ❐ Identify different writing styles, formatting, and winning strategies

Listed below are the names of the grant writers, their affiliations, and the name of the funding agency.

1. Application to the 21st Century Community Learning Centers Program, Project Writers—Pat Conner and Marijo Lewis with the help and advice of others, Sumner County Schools, Gallatin, Tennessee

Application to the 21st Century Community Learning Centers Program

Application for Federal Education Assistance		Note: If available, please provide application package on diskette and specify the file format	U.S. Department of Education Form Approved OMB No. 1875-0106 Exp. 06/30/2001

Applicant Information

1. Name and Address

Legal Name: _Sumner County Board of Education_

Address: _225 East Main Street_

Organizational Unit

Sumner County Board of Education

Gallatin	**TN**	_Sumner_	37066 _- 2908_
City	State	County	ZIP Code + 4

2. Applicant's D-U-N-S Number: |0 |6 |9 |0 |9 |5 |9 |9 |0 |

3. Applicant's T-I-N |6 |2 | - |0 |6 |8 |1 |0 |6 |4 |

4. Catalog of Federal Domestic Assistance #: 84. 2| 8| 7| A| →

5. Project Director: _Pat Conner_

Address: _225 East Main Street_

Gallatin	_TN_	_37066_ _2908_
City	State	Zip code + 4

Tel. #: (615) _451_ - _6500_   Fax #: (615) _451-6518_

E-Mail Address: _Connorp@ k12tn.net_

6. Is the applicant delinquent on any Federal debt? ___ Yes _X_ No
(If "Yes," attach an explanation.)

Title: 21st Century Community Learning Centers

7. Type of Applicant *(Enter appropriate letter in the box.)* | B |

A - State	H - Independent School District
B - County	I - Public College or University
C - Municipal	J - Private, Non-Profit College or University
D - Township	K - Indian Tribe
E - Interstate	L - Individual
F - Intermunicipal	M - Private, Profit-Making Organization
G - Special District	N - Other *(Specify):* _____

8. Novice Applicant ___ Yes _X_ No

Application Information

9. Type of Submission:

-PreApplication	-Application
___ Construction	___ Construction
___ Non-Construction	_X_ Non-Construction

10. Is application subject to review by Executive Order 12372 process?

___ Yes *(Date made available to the Executive Order 12372 process for review):* ___ / ___ / _____

_X_ No *(If "No," check appropriate box below.)*
   ___ Program is not covered by E.O. 12372.
   ___ Program has not been selected by State for review.

11. Proposed Project Dates: _7_ / _1_ / _00_   _6_ / _30_ / _01_

Start Date:	End Date:

12. Are any research activities involving human subjects planned at any time during the proposed project period? _x_ Yes ___ No

a. If "Yes," Exemption(s) #: _____   b. Assurance of Compliance #:

_____   *OR*   None

c. IRB approval date: _____   ___ Full IRB **or**
_____   ___ Expedited Review

13. Descriptive Title of Applicant's Project:

UNITY.COM Learning Center will offer after-school and evening activities to students and families at three selected middle schools.

Estimated Funding

14a. Federal	$ _390,012_	. 00
b. Applicant	$ _____	. 00
c. State	$ _____	. 00
d. Local	$ _177,911_	. 00
e. Other	$ _____	. 00
f. Program Income	$ _____	. 00
g. TOTAL	$ _567,923_	. 00

Authorized Representative Information

15. To the best of my knowledge and belief, all data in this preapplication/application are true and correct. The document has been duly authorized by the governing body of the applicant and the applicant will comply with the attached assurances if the assistance is awarded.

a. Typed Name of Authorized Representative

Merrol N. Hyde

b. Title: _Director of Schools_

c. Tel. #: (615) _451_ - _5200_   Fax #: (615) _451_ - _6518_

d. E-Mail Address: _helbigj@ k12tn.net_

e. Signature of Authorized Representative

_____   Date: ___ / ___

ED 424 (rev 11/12/99)

21

90

TABLE OF CONTENTS

(5) <u>QUALITY OF PROJECT EVALUATION</u>

  (A) The extent to which the methods of evaluation include the use of objective performance measures that are clearly related to the intended outcomes of the project and will produce quantitative and qualitative data 15

BUDGET AND BUDGET NARRATIVE

ASSURANCES

APPENDIX A

PROGRAM SUMMARY AND ABSTRACT

Name and address of applicant: **Contact Information:**

Sumner County Board of Education   Pat Conner, Coordinator
225 East Main Street   Safe & Drug Free Schools
Gallatin, TN 37066   Phone: (615) 451-6500 Fax: (615) 451-6518
                                          e-mail: Connorp@k12tn.net

Program title: **UNITY.COM** Learning Center Program

This program will serve: 1 rural public school   2 inner city public schools

The applicant intends to provide services within the following Empowerment Zone or Enterprise Community (identify if applicable):

Please provide the name of each school that will have a Community Learning Center:

Rucker Stewart Middle School, Shafer Middle School, Westmoreland Middle School

In the schools to be served (please provide the totals for all schools):

Number of students served **400 minimum**; Community members served **150 minimum**; Grade levels served **6-8**; Students who are: eligible for free or reduced-price lunch **36%**; Limited English proficient **.02%**

Program Abstract:

     UNITY.COM Learning Center Program will establish an extended day and year program that will operate from 3:00-6:00pm Monday through Friday for students and from 5:30-8:00pm for families. In the second and third years, four one week specialty camps will be held during the summer from 9:00 to Noon Monday through Friday. The program responds to the identified needs of our community, most specifically underachievement in Math, the Social Sciences, and written expression; high rates of violence and substance abuse; rural isolation; low neighborhood attachment; lack of parent support and involvement; poor attendance; and, discipline problems. **UNITY.COM** is a collaborative effort among the school system, over twelve community organizations, and parents and volunteers that will serve a minimum of 400 students and 150 parents from three "high need" middle schools in Sumner County. **UNITY.COM** has three primary goals: to increase students' abilities to achieve at national and state standards in Social Sciences (Science and Social Studies), Math, and Written Expression; to reduce the number of students involved in self destructive behaviors such as alcohol and drugs and violence; and, to increase parent and family support and involvement at each school site. These goals will be met through a program that includes a strong connection with classroom teachers and an assessment of each student's individual strengths and challenges. Students will be able to participate in experiential activities that support academic achievement. These activities include a strong technology component, the arts, service learning, counseling, and various other non-traditional methods. The intended outcomes for the program will reflect the accomplishment of the goals and will be measured through increases in TCAP scores, attendance rates, positive behavioral changes, and decreases in positive attitudes towards alcohol, tobacco, and other drug use.

PROGRAM NARRATIVE

(1) NEED FOR PROJECT

(A)   The extent to which the proposed project will provide services or otherwise address the needs of students at risk of educational failure.

Sarah, a 14-year-old in a single-parent household, enters a chat room one afternoon that leads to danger. She has no idea that the boy she is chatting with is a 33-year-old pedophile who talks her into inviting him over when her mom isn't home. Tyrone, a 7th grade African American male, meets up with his homeboys after school to go fight another rival group at a local apartment complex. Jesse, a 6th grade white female, is failing in math and science due in large part to her below grade level reading ability. Because of her sense of failure, her behavior at school is disruptive and her attendance is sporadic. These are real stories of young people in Sumner County who would benefit from a comprehensive after-school program that focuses on academics, recreation and the arts.

In the 1970s parents worried about their children getting involved with sex, drugs, and rock 'n roll. Twenty-first century parents still have those same concerns along with the threat of AIDS, suicide, stress, safety issues, and the Internet.

When school lets out in Sumner County, thousands of middle school students go home to an empty house and spend three or more hours unsupervised. The hours after school are a vulnerable time for middle school aged children who are too old for traditional daycare services yet not mature enough for working parents to feel comfortable about leaving them at home alone. Many students either turn on the television for entertainment, surf the Net, or meet up with their friends, which often leads to trouble.

Sumner County is primarily an urban community located in Middle Tennessee, adjacent to Nashville. The seventh largest county in the state with a total population of 117,000, 20.5% of that population is youth ages 5-17. Sumner County is a diverse county comprised of five very distinct communities. These include Hendersonville, a suburban community whose residents primarily commute to Nashville; Gallatin and White House, both urban communities; and Portland and Westmoreland, primarily rural communities. The mean per capita income is $19,694,00.

The Sumner County school system has a total of 39 schools, 6 high schools, 9 middle schools, 22 elementary schools, 1 alternative school, and 1 full-time night high school. The total student population is 22,360, of that number 5,300 are middle school students. Currently in Sumner County, all 22 elementary schools have before and after-school programs operated by either the YMCA or by the school themselves through the Department of Children Services. There *are* organized, stimulating activities available through school and community organizations

1

for middle school students—sports, special interest clubs, dance, music and art programs—but only a small percentage of students participate. Many young people choose not to participate because they either can't afford the fees associated with some of the programs, they're convinced they wouldn't enjoy these opportunities, or they have no parent to transport them to and from the activity. This in no way diminishes the "wish" or need for after-school programs by many middle school aged children and their families. The desire for structured, educational after-school programs is strong and the need is even greater.

The need for after-school programming was more than evident this fall when, as part of the annual Sumner County Teen Issues Survey, middle school students were asked the question, "Where do you most often smoke cigarettes?" they answered, "At home when no one is there." When asked the question, "Where do you most often drink alcohol?" they answered, "At a friend's house or at home when no one is there." The survey also showed that 27.4% of middle school students smoke cigarettes on a regular basis, 23% drink alcohol, and the average age to first use was 12, or 6th grade. In a community where 73% of parents work full-time, the answers to these questions were every parent's nightmare come true.

Not only is there a concern about drug use by middle school aged children in Sumner County, there is a concern about incidents of violence. Teen Issues Survey results showed that 30% of middle school students were afraid that another student would harm them either at or after school and 19% were actually hurt by one of their peers. Middle school administrators are reporting an increase in the number of reported fights after school hours, not on school property, but at the homes of students whose parents are not there.

Juvenile crime statistics across the nation show that the majority of juvenile crime occurs between the hours of 3:00-7:00pm. Juvenile crime statistics for Sumner County reflect the same trend. When asked if they have ever gotten in trouble with the police, 10.1% of middle school students answered **"yes."**

Another disturbing statistic has emerged from the Teen Issues Survey. Middle school students were asked, "Have you ever thought about committing suicide?" 14.2% or 694 students answered **"Yes."** This is an extremely high number for any age group. This statistic is being addressed across the county at all middle schools and it will be addressed in the proposed after-school programs as well.

While all nine middle schools in Sumner County would benefit from an after-school program, three "high need" middle schools were selected as sites for this grant application. The schools selected are: Rucker-Stewart Middle School (RMS), Shafer Middle School (SMS), and

Westmoreland Middle School (WMS). RMS, student population 518, and SMS, student population 750, are located in Gallatin. Gallatin, an urban community, is the county seat and is home to 80% of the county's minority population. It is also the site of the housing projects, which both schools serve. WMS, student population 365, is located in Westmoreland in upper northern Sumner County and borders the Kentucky line. Westmoreland is the smallest community in Sumner County and has only one major industry – agriculture. Due to its location, Westmoreland is isolated from the other communities of Sumner County and has very limited access to health and social services. This rural isolation has also led to increased rates of alcohol and drug use.

These schools were selected based on their location in the county, the information gathered from the Teen Issues Survey, their low academic achievement scores, and on the needs assessments conducted by the advisory groups that have been formed at each middle school. The following tables outline some of the data utilized in the selection process:

	RMS	SMS	WMS
% of students who don't live with both parents	48%	46%	43%
% of students whose parents didn't graduate H.S.	13%	20%	27%
% of students on free and reduced lunch	31%	42%	34%
% of population that is minority	31%	25%	7%
% of parents who work full-time	72%	71%	76%
% of students who contemplated suicide	16%	16%	16%
% of students who don't participate in school activities	29%	28%	36%
% of students who miss 1-3 days of school a month	50%	54%	55%

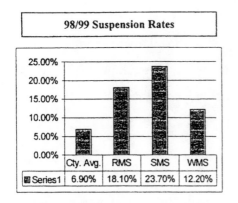

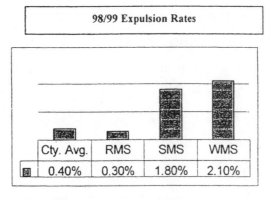

Of the nine middle schools in Sumner County, SMS ranks first in suspensions and second in expulsions, RMS ranks second in suspensions and fourth in expulsions, and WMS ranks fourth in suspensions and first in expulsions.

Each of the three selected middle schools has an active advisory group that has just completed a comprehensive needs assessment. Teachers, parents, community members, and students were asked to identify the top five needs of their respective schools. The top five needs

3

for each school can be categorized as follows: (1) family support/parenting programs; (2) enhance social skills of students; (3) funding for programs; (4) motivation of staff and students; and, (5) drug, alcohol and violence prevention.

The risk factors and needs identified at each school have a significant impact on student achievement. With instructional programs in Sumner County all being equal in quality and design, the students in the three selected schools are failing to make comparable academic gains. The following chart shows how all three selected schools are below the national average in performance level proficiency as measured by the Tennessee Comprehensive Assessment Program (TCAP).

| | National Average | | | SMS | | | RMS | | | WMS | | |
	6th	7th	8th	6th	7th	8th	6th	7th	8th	6th	7th	8th
Math	12	21	35	7	22	**29**	**6**	35	35	**9**	**14**	39
Science	14	26	34	**11**	27	37	14	35	30	**10**	**16**	37
Soc. Stu.	21	29	35	**16**	**24**	35	**20**	36	41	21	**20**	**32**

WMS and SMS are below the Sumner County percentile rank in every TCAP subject in every grade. RMS is below the Sumner County percentile rank in every TCAP subject in 6th and 8th grade. RMS and SMS were below the state and national average in writing proficiency as measured by TCAP in 1998 and 1999. Academic activities for math, social sciences, and writing will be a major focus in the after-school program.

As evidenced by the above data, all three selected schools would benefit tremendously from a range of quality, educational, developmental, and recreational after-school services. We are proposing to offer these services to students and their families through the **UNITY.COM** Learning Center Program. **UNITY.COM** will involve not only students and their families but the community as well. We are excited about the many possibilities **UNITY.COM** has to offer our students.

(2) QUALITY OF PROJECT DESIGN

(A)   The extent to which the goals, objectives, and outcomes are clear and measurable.

The mission of the Sumner County school system is to provide all students a safe environment in which they are given challenging, learning opportunities that will foster responsibility, and help for students to grow into productive and respectful citizens. The proposed **UNITY.COM** Learning Center Program supports the mission of the school system by offering students and their families expanded opportunities to participate in educational, developmental, and recreational services through after-school and evening activities. **All students and their families at the selected schools will be encouraged to participate.**

Based on the identified needs of the three selected schools and the performance indicators for 21st Century Community Learning Centers, the following goals, objectives, and strategies have been developed for the successful development, implementation, and evaluation of **UNITY.COM.**

GOAL ONE:

By June 30, 2001, the schools participating in **UNITY.COM** will achieve a 2% gain in the number of students scoring in the proficient and higher performance levels as measured by the Tennessee Comprehensive Assessment Program (TCAP).

Objective One:

To develop and implement after-school academic activities to increase students' abilities to achieve at national and state standards in Social Sciences (Social Studies and Science), Math, and Written Expression as measured by a 2% gain in the number of students scoring in the proficient or higher levels on the TCAP.

Strategies:

1. Recruit, hire and train one full-time director and three site managers at each **UNITY.COM** site to coordinate after-school activities, supervise program staff, solicit community volunteers, and to develop community partnerships to enhance the program.

2. Recruit, hire and train a lead teacher and assistants at each **UNITY.COM** site to coordinate after school academic study programs in the areas of Math, Language Arts, and Social Sciences (Science and Social Studies). One teacher and a tutor will be hired in each subject area for each site and will be responsible for:

   A. Assessing each individual student's performance level in each subject area using TCAP test results;

   B. Using TCAP scores, identifying specific learning objectives for each student in their subject are of need;

   C. Designing an individual program of study for each student in those subject areas of need;

   D. Receiving appropriate training on computer software programs (Accelerated Math, Plato Solutions) to be integrated into each subject area;

   E. Providing instruction for preparation for administration of TCAP testing;

F.   Coordinating Socratic Seminars once a week to integrate writing and social science objectives;

G.   Provide authentic assessment opportunities to demonstrate understanding of math, writing proficiency, or social sciences according to NCTM Standards;

H.   Evaluation of student progress using pre and post assessment;

I.   Reporting to regular classroom teacher on academic progress of each student; and,

J.   Coordinating student and parent conferences to discuss academic progress.

3.   Recruit and hire three technology specialists, one for each **UNITY.COM** site, to coordinate and conduct computer lab after-school and evening activities for students and families:

4.   Recruit and hire three librarians, one for each **UNITY.COM** site, to coordinate after-school activities for students and families.

5.   Recruit and hire three Related Arts teachers, one for each **UNITY.COM** site, to conduct after-school activities in the arts. Activities include: music, art, drama, cooking, sewing.

GOAL TWO:

By June 30, 2001, the number of students participating in **UNITY.COM** who exhibit a positive attitude toward alcohol and drugs and other self-destructive behaviors will be decreased by 3% as evidenced by survey instruments developed by the program evaluation team.

Objective One:

To reduce by 3% the number of students participating in **UNITY.COM** after-school activities who report a favorable attitude towards alcohol, tobacco, and other drugs as evidenced by survey instruments developed by the program evaluation team.

Objective Two:

To reduce by 3% the number of students participating in **UNITY.COM** after-school activities who exhibit disruptive and violent behaviors as measured by survey instruments developed by the program evaluation team.

Objective Three:

To reduce by 3% the number of students participating in **UNITY.COM** after-school activities who report a positive attitude towards violence and suicide as measured by survey instruments developed by the program evaluation team.

Strategies:

1. Recruit and hire three certified counselors, one for each **UNITY.COM** site, who will be responsible for the following:

   A. The development and implementation of an alcohol, drug, and violence prevention program to include drug information, conflict resolution, and social skill development;

   B. Individual and group counseling sessions for students;

   C. Counseling and referral services for families;

   D. Communicate with school personnel about student progress; and,

   E. Coordinate service learning opportunities within the community;

GOAL THREE:

By June 30, 2001, there will be a 2% increase in the number of parents, families, and community members who support drug and violence prevention education and after-school activities at the three selected school sites.

Objective One:

UNITY.COM will increase by 5% the number of parents and families involved in after-school programs at the three selected school sites through participation in a range of high-quality educational, developmental, and recreational services as measured by survey instruments developed by the evaluation team.

Objective Two:

UNITY.COM will increase by 5% the number of parents and families who volunteer at the three selected school sites as measured by survey instruments developed by the evaluation team.

Objective Three:

UNITY.COM will increase by 5% the number of community organizations who support and are involved in the three selected school sites through the establishment of partnerships that promote collaboration and aid in the planning, implementation, and sustainability of after-school programs as measured by survey instruments developed by the evaluation team.

Strategies:

1. Develop and implement a comprehensive parent component to include the following:

   A. Parenting programs;

   B. GED, ESL, and Family Literacy programs;

   C. Access to counseling and referral services;

     D.   Computer/Internet workshops.

2.   Recruit parent volunteers to work at each program site to assist as follows:

     A.   Tutoring/Mentoring;

     B.   Chaperone for field trips; and,

     C.   Any activities associated with the daily operations of the program.

3.   Establish linkages with community organizations to provide quality after-school activities/programs. Activities/programs to include, but not limited to:

     A.   Music, visual arts, drama programs;

     B.   Radio production;

     C.   Cultural diversity programs;

     D.   First-aid training, baby-sitting certification, HIV-AIDS education;

     E.   Swimming, physical conditioning, and recreational activities, intramural sports;

     F.   Mentoring; intergenerational program; academic tutoring in all subject areas;

     H.   Alcohol, drug, and violence prevention programs;

     I.   ESL program;

     J.   Adult Basic Education classes to include GED and family literacy;

     K.   Strengthening Families parent/children program;

     L.   Health risk assessments, health education classes;

     M.   Computer/Internet skills courses; and,

     N.   Family field trips and service learning opportunities

(B)   **Extent to which the design of the project will successfully address the needs.**

The advisory groups at each of the three selected school sites have gone to great lengths to ensure that the needs identified at their schools will be addressed by the **UNITY.COM** Learning Center Program. These needs are specifically addressed in the measurable goals, objectives, and strategies and can be read as follows: (1) Academic underachievement in Math, the Social Sciences, and Written Expression; (2) High rates of violence and other self-destructive behaviors; (3) High percentage of suspensions and expulsions; (4) High rates of alcohol, tobacco, and other drug use; (5) Lack of parental support and involvement; (6) Rural isolation and lack of available services; (7) High number of students from single parent homes; (8) High number of students where both parents work; and, (9) Lack of student motivation.

UNITY.COM will offer students and their families programs and activities that will address all these identified needs. Open from 3:00-6:00 pm five days a week, not including weekend family field trips, the proposed project will serve a minimum of 150 students respectively at RMS and SMS and a minimum of 100 students at WMS. Family participation should average around 50 parents per school site.

The staff will involve students in educational activities to improve their abilities in the areas of Math, the Social Sciences, and Writing Expression through not only tutorial assistance but creative projects such as *Socratic Seminars*. A strong technology component will be integrated into every subject area as well. Research-based programs that have been proven to be effective in reducing or preventing alcohol and drug use and violence will be offered as well as programs in art, music, drama, cultural diversity, service learning, intramural sports, swimming and physical conditioning. And, students will benefit from individual and group counseling with a certified counselor who will be there to address their emotional needs. The educational and social benefits for students will be evaluated through positive gains in academics and attendance and in observable behavioral changes.

Families participating in afternoon or evening activities at each **UNITY.COM** will benefit from a wide range of educational, developmental, and recreational services. These activities include parenting programs, technology literacy classes, adult education classes, health risk assessments and other health services, and counseling and referral services. Family activities will be held from 5:30 - 8:30 pm.

In order to be successful, **UNITY.COM** must meet the needs identified at each school. We feel that we have been successful in not only identifying the needs of our schools but in the development of a comprehensive after-school program to effectively meet the needs of the students.

YEARS TWO AND THREE

In years two and three, **UNITY.COM** Learning Center will increase the number of students served, provide additional parent training sessions, and sponsor a series of summer camps. Funding for the additional programs will come from two sources: (1) analysis of individual school budgets to redistribute funds (i.e.,Title I, Title II, TitleVI, Extended Contract funds, and school grants); and (2) one-time grant funds (computer, nonconsumable materials). The summer camps will use blended units where students explore levels of science, math, and writing expression by use of technology. Students will be involved in adventure-based activities designed to boost self-esteem. Cultural and recreational units will be integrated according to students interest level. The Gallatin Civic Center, YMCA, and Global Education Center will assist in providing activities for the students. Summer camp hours will be from 9:00 – 12:00 am.

(C)   Extent to which the proposed project will establish linkages.

The Sumner County school system is a member of the Sumner County Health Council. The Health Council was formed by the Tennessee Department of Health to assess the "health" of Sumner County and to develop a plan of action to address the needs of the community. The Health Council is comprised of persons from area hospitals, social services agencies, local businesses, and private citizens. With the assistance of the Sumner County Health Council and through the advisory groups established at each school site, **UNITY.COM** Learning Center will establish extensive partnerships with numerous community organizations to provide services to the targeted population. These partnerships represent a commitment by the community to the health and education of students involved in **UNITY.COM.** The chart below shows the services/activities community agencies and organizations have specifically committed to in association with **UNITY.COM** Learning Center.

ACA = ACADEMICS	AED = ADULT EDUCATION	ADCD = ARTS, DRAMA, CULTURAL DIVERSITY
CS = COMMUNITY SERVICE	FAMH = FAMILY HEALTH	REC = RECREATION
TU = TUTORS/MENTORS	TEC = TECHNOLOGY	

Organization	Component	Services
Sumner County Schools	ACA	Math, *Socratic* Writing Seminars, Social Sciences; Related Arts
Volunteer State Community College	ACA	*MathCounts*, writing skills, radio production; all-male chorus for at-risk
Sumner County Schools	AED	Adult Education classes ; GED & ESL program
Gallatin Arts Brd. /Art Resources of TN – Sumner	ADCD	Family Arts Program; "Character" art education; city building murals; middle-school murals
Steeple Players	ADCD	Drama skills, playwright structure, & improvisation
Family Resource Center	ADCD	Cultural programs for the family – workshops & dinners
Global Education Center	ADCD	International percussion & dance; Multicultural education; Therapeutic writing
Mid.TN Girl Scouts	ADCD	*Herminatas'*- ESL leadership program for Hispanic girls
American Heart	CS	Jump rope for heart demonstrations; Double-Dutch Teams

YMCA	CS	Service learning program and an environmental program
Juvenile Justice System	FAMH	***Strengthening Families*** - Court ordered program for families of substance abuse
Alcohol & Drug Council of Middle TN	FAMH	Family alcohol & drug prevention workshops; Student-assistance counseling; ***Strengthening Families*** facilitation
Sumner County Health Dept.	FAMH	Health risk assessments; first-aid training; baby-sitting certification; nutrition, HIV-AIDS and health related classes
Sumner County Safe & Drug Free Schools	FAMH	***Character Education*** & research based ***Lifeskills curriculum***
Gallatin Civic Center	REC	Junior lifeguard safety; swimming; physical conditioning; basketball
Middle School Coaches	REC	Intramural sports – volleyball; softball; football
Volunteer State College	TU	Mentors/tutors for instruction & homework assistance
Gallatin Senior Citizen Center	TU	Mentor & Intergenerational Program – to foster special ties between students and seniors – baking, sing-along,
High School students	TU	Teachers assistants and pre-school care for ***Strengthening Families***
Middle School Teachers	TEC	Computer/Internet courses; technology learning; research based ***Here's Looking At You*** drug & alcohol prevention program; cooking, and baking.

(3) ADEQUACY OF RESOURCES

(A) Support provided by applicant organization.

The three school sites, RMS, SMS, and WMS, that will house the proposed **UNITY.COM** Learning Center Program all have adequate space to accommodate after-school activities. RMS and SMS are fairly new facilities, having been built within the past five years, and at WMS an additional wing has been added within the past three years. All three schools are fully accessible to persons with disabilities and have the following areas available for activities: large, indoor gymnasium and outdoor sports area for recreation/games; stage area for drama/music productions and other programs; cafeteria/commons area for snacks, meetings, and any large activities; individual classrooms and guidance office for tutoring and counseling; a large, well-equipped library; and, a large computer lab with 30-35 computers with Internet access for use with students and parents. Each program site will also have access to all available equipment at each school.

This may include recreational equipment, televisions and VCRs, use of cafeteria equipment, and of course, telephone and fax equipment.

The state of Tennessee, through its Extended Contact program, will provide funding to compensate teachers who work with students outside the regular school hours. Each school site will use these teachers who work with students outside the regular school hours. **UNITY.COM** will also take advantage of the resources provided by federally funded programs within the school district. These include Title I, Title II, Title VI, Goals 2000, and Safe and Drug Free Schools. These programs will provide in-kind services to include materials and training. The Safe and Drug Free Schools Program will also make available the services of the two full-time Middle School Coordinators that serve the selected schools. These coordinators will assist in program development and implementation.

In addition to utilizing the school facilities and equipment, all three school sites will use the available resources provided by community partners. Examples are Volunteer State Community College and the Gallatin Civic Center. The Civic Center has an Olympic-size pool, indoor gymnasium, conditioning track, exercise room, racquetball courts, and meeting rooms that can be used for instructional purposes. Students will be involved in a junior lifeguard program, basketball, volleyball, and conditioning activities. At Volunteer State, students will receive hands-on experience in the writing and production of a radio show in their on-campus radio station. Sumner County is fortunate to have community partners supporting its goals for student success.

(B)   The extent to which the costs are reasonable to the number of persons served.

The total direct program cost for **UNITY.COM** for the first year is $390,012. The total proposed program will serve a minimum of 400 students and 150 parents in activities during the school year. The cost per participant is minimal—approximately $780.00.

We feel that the families should make an investment in the program. For that reason, a one time fee of $20.00 will be charged to those families who will be participating in the **UNITY.COM** program, with scholarships available to students who are on free and reduced lunch program. All other activities will be free of charge, including Strengthening Families.

The proposed budget will ensure that the efficient implementation of the goals, objectives, and strategies at each program site is accomplished and that caring, competent professionals are involved who understand the needs of the students and their families. The costs allocated allow for lower teacher/client ratios (approximately 1:10)—an important step in improving, not only, academic achievement, behavior, and attendance for students, but family relations as well. The program and its budget costs are relatively small when compared to the potential impact this program has on success.

Future sources of funding for the after-school program will be sought from the community groups, United Way, additional grant opportunities, and from the parents of students served by the program.

(4)   QUALITY OF MANAGEMENT PLAN

(A)   Adequacy of the plan to achieve the project objectives.

The organization structure for the **UNITY.COM** Learning Center lead staff consists of a project director, a middle school coordinator, a site manager, and lead teacher. The team will work together to prevent or resolve problems with a central system in place that allows school personnel and **UNITY.COM** administrators to have an easy back and forth relationship with accountability to all partners. Weekly staff meetings will ensure that the goals, objectives, and strategies are being met at each site.

The Middle School Coordinator (MSC) will be the connection between the school system and the partners in the community. The MSC will assist the program staff in locating and securing volunteers to assist as tutors, mentors, music and recreation assistants. The MSC will monitor the program on a regular basis to ensure that all components are in place, gather feedback, and offer recommendations for improvement.

The Project Director (PD) will provide leadership direction to keep activities connected to the goals, at all three sites. The PD will possess a masters degree in administration. The supervisory position requires strong interpersonal skills; evidence of leadership; interdisciplinary teaching and learning; innovative teaching skills; and knowledge of the community.

The qualifications for the Site Manager (SM) requires a bachelors degree. The SM provides a system of communication with scheduled activities; volunteer schedules and maintains parent contact.

The Lead Teacher is responsible for the activities and programs at each center. Qualifications include teacher certification, employment at the site, strong teamwork and leadership skills. Sumner County certified teachers and retirees will be hired as instructors and assistants. Community personnel and high school students will be hired as assistants with sports programs and preschool care for the *Strengthening Families* component.

13

The certified counselor will be experienced in individual and group facilitation with alcohol, tobacco, and other drug knowledge. Other professionals outside the school system will be contracted to deliver specialized services for the **UNITY.COM** Learning Center.

A core group of students and faculty from the local college and high school and the local senior citizens will be interviewed, selected, and trained. This intergenerational program creates a wonderful bond between generations.

Additional volunteers will be secured from parents, corporate sponsors, and civic clubs to serve as mentors and tutor assistants. These volunteers will be interviewed, selected and trained with the assistance of Volunteer State College and the advisory board.

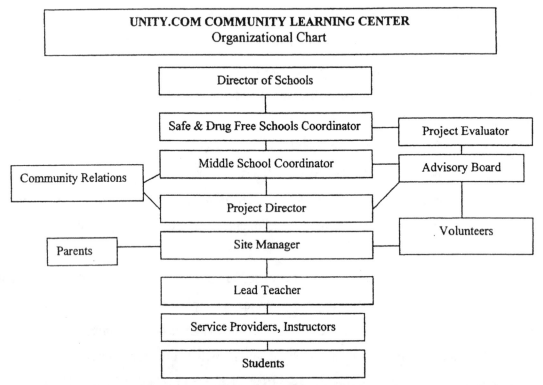

(B)   Diversity of perspectives brought to bear in project operation.

An advisory board exists at each site comprised of students, parents, community members, and school staff to ensure program diversity. The focus of each advisory group is to assess the needs of the school and the community by developing, conducting, and analyzing an extensive needs assessment; by participating in the selection of effective programs and implementation; by assisting in program evaluation; and, acting as an advocate in seeking support from the community monetarily and in the spirit of volunteerism for the **UNITY.COM** Learning Center.

MONTH	UNITY.COM LEARNING CENTER TIMELINE
July	Announce the award of the grant in newspaper; staff recruitment and selection of Project Director; development of policies and procedures, development of curriculum ; meet with evaluator; volunteer recruitment, brochures developed
August	Continued curriculum development and staff recruitment, staff training; volunteer training; recruitment of students; lead staff meeting; weekly staff meetings; evaluator meeting
September	Ongoing recruitment of students and families; after school program begins; truancy program begins; Strengthening Families recruitment; advisory board meeting; weekly staff meetings
October	Staff development; evaluator meeting; weekly staff meetings; ideas for summer program
November	Program services; family field-trip; weekly staff meetings; start planning summer program
December	Complete plans for summer and make promotional material; mid-year evaluations complete ; weekly staff meetings; program services break for holidays
January	Program services resume; distribute summer program brochures; weekly staff meetings resume; ATOD distribute pre-tests for second semester
February	Second semester Strengthening Families evening program begins; staff training; target new grants
March	Continue summer recruitment; program services continue; weekly staff meetings; meet with evaluators; grants written & submitted; planning and recruitment for following year
April	Program services continue; weekly staff meetings; grant writing; continued planning for following year
May	Post test evaluations done; after school program ends; final reports written, program evaluations
June	Start summer program; complete evaluations and submit to proper authority; weekly staff meetings

(5) QUALITY OF PROJECT EVALUATION

(A)   Objective performance measures used by project evaluation plan.

The evaluation of the proposed project will be performed as an integral part of the implementation. Both process and outcome issues will be addressed. The evaluation will be tied to ongoing program review and planning through the use of an evaluation team that will include the project director and the middle school coordinator.

Types of Data to Be Collected: The extent to which the proposed programs are developed and implemented will be evaluated, including the number and nature of participants. Process data will include:

- Description of programs implemented
- Type of services offered including core educational services
- Quality of services
- Number of extended hours
- Problems encountered during grant period and solutions tried
- Number of students and parents who participate in programs

Outcome data will include:

- Baseline and post program TCAP scores

- Baseline and post program grades
- Baseline and post program student progress on math, social sciences, and writing expression as measured by teachers on report cards
- Baseline and post program student school attendance
- Baseline and post program student disciplinary procedures
- Baseline and post program survey data of student attitudes toward alcohol, tobacco, and other drug use; rebelliousness; school; and family relationships using the Student Attitudinal Inventory (Kim, 1981)
- Baseline and annual counts of the number of parents families, and community organizations that contribute time, money, or other resources to the program
- Participant satisfaction with the program
- Baseline and post program student behavior as reported by teachers on report cards

When Data Will Be Collected: Data will be collected from the beginning of the project to be used in both process and outcome evaluations. Data needed for the Threshold Gating Model and process evaluation will be collected throughout the program. Baseline data related to time and resources parents, families, and community organizations contribute to the target schools will be collected prior to the implementation of the program. Individual level data, such as attitudes, grades and behavior will be collected prior to each participant's admission to the program and again when the individual completes the program.

Methods: The evaluation will use the Threshold Gating approach described by Kim, Crutchfield, Williams, and Hepler (1994). This approach allows active participation in the evaluation by non-evaluation staff and partners. The approach also offers a sufficient number of logical nets with which to negate alternative generalizations. The approach assumes that a program cannot be effective until all major components of the program are successfully completed in a cumulative fashion. Using the Threshold Gating Approach, the evaluation team consisting of key program staff and the evaluator will specify the intermediate outcomes which must be achieved for the successful completion of the project. Each major component will then be evaluated for its successful completion. This evaluation is conducted concurrently with the implementation of the project. Results of the evaluation will be use to determine whether the project team should continue to each next step in implementation or whether the project team should continue to each next step in implementation or whether adjustments need to be made before continuing. This approach uses quantitative and qualitative methods to observe and describe the implementation of the proposed project from its conception through the completion of the federally funded period.

The evaluation team will set each threshold prior to implementation, using established research findings to determine thresholds. Accepted evaluation methodologies will then be selected to measure each threshold. The evaluator will then use these methodologies to determine whether each threshold has been met. Some of the anticipated evaluation methodologies are described below:

- Analysis of archival evidence produced by program staff, such as meeting minutes, training, agendas, and other communications with staff, to describe the progress of the project.
- Program staff, teacher, and student satisfaction surveys to determine the quality of implementation.
- Social accounting, that is, keeping records of the number of participants, to determine the number of people trained.

These methodologies are already used by the Sumner County Safe and Drug Free Schools program for similar programs and will be adapted for the proposed program. These are all the methodologies anticipated at this time for the process and outcome evaluations; but since the methodology must be appropriate for the threshold, others may need to to be developed to determine whether the thresholds have been met. The Threshold Gating Approach has been used by the proposed evaluation team in the past to evaluate the three year funded Sumner County Drug Free Schools Personnel Training Grant and is being used currently to evaluate the Middle School Coordinators Grant.

Instruments: Program staff will adapt satisfaction instruments for students, parents or family members, and community members from satisfaction survey instruments that are currently being used by the Sumner County Board of Education to make them program specific. The satisfaction instruments will measure the benefit, quality, and enjoyment of the program. Program staff will develop an instrument to assess the students academic ability with regard to math, social studies, and writing expression. Evaluation staff will adapt an observation/interview instrument to assess the quality of the programs from similar instruments that have been used previously by the lead evaluator to assess the quality to educational programs. Instruments will be developed and adapted in fall, 2000 prior to the implementation of the program.

Analysis Procedures: Analysis procedures will vary depending on the type of data. Both qualitative and quantitative procedures will be used. The process will investigate how well the program was implemented. Major questions that will be answered by the process evaluation include "How effectively was the program implemented?" and "What is the level of quality of the program?" Qualitative procedures will be used to describe program implementation including successes and barriers. Social accounting procedures will be used to collect, analyze, and report the types of services, numbers of extended hours and number of participants. The Quality of Program survey and observation data will be analyzed using both quantitative data reduction strategies such as means and qualitative strategies.

The major purpose of the outcome evaluation is to determine whether objectives were met. The following hypotheses will be tested:

H1: The schools participating in the program will report a 2% gain in the numbers of students scoring in the proficient and higher performance levels on the Social Sciences, Math, and Written Expression scales of the Tennessee Comprehensive Assessment Program (TCAP).

H2: The number of students participating in **UNITY.COM** who exhibit a positive attitude toward alcohol and drugs and other self-destructive behaviors will decrease by 3%.

H3: The number of students participating in **UNITY.COM** who exhibit disruptive and violent behaviors will be reduced by 3%.

H4: The number of students participating in **UNITY.COM** who report a positive attitude toward violence will be reduced by 3%.

H5: There will be a 5% increase in the number of parents and family members who participate in programs offered by the school.

H6: There will be a 5% increase in the number of parents and family members who volunteer at the school.

H7: There will be a 5% increase in the number of community organizations who support the school with volunteers and resources.

Hypothesis 1 will be tested by comparing the baseline (spring, 2000) number of students in each school who score proficient and higher performance levels of the TCAP. The percent of students from baseline to outcome will be calculated. Hypotheses 2 through 4 will be tested by comparing the number of students reporting positive attitudes on the post survey. The percent of students from baseline to outcome will be calculated. Hypothesis 2 will be further tested by conducting matched t-tests to determine whether there is statistically significant difference between pre and posttest means. There will be sufficient statistical power for this statistical analysis. Hypotheses 5 through 7 will be tested by comparing baseline participation rates to outcome participation rates and calculating the differences.

Use of Evaluation Results to Monitor Progress and Provide Accountability is integral to the Threshold Gating Approach. The evaluators will provide quarterly reports to the evaluation team that document program successes, unmet needs, barriers, and problems encountered in planning and implementing services. These quarterly reports will then be used to make adjustments in the program to improve the quality of the program. At the end of the project, the evaluation team will prepare a final report that discusses the impact of the successes, barriers, etc. on the final outcomes of the project. The report will also include information about the specific intervention provided including when, how often and where the intervention was provided; and how and what data were collected. Finally, the report will discuss any changes or adjustments made to the project to overcome barriers, solve problems and enhance success.

Protection of Human Subjects. Care will be taken to protect the confidentiality of the data. All reports will give summary information, no individual level data.

Qualifications of the Evaluators. Nancy Hepler, Ph.D., will lead the evaluation team for the proposed project. The other evaluation team members will include Ms. Pat Conner, the Sumner County Safe and Drug Free Schools Coordinator; the second evaluator, Jean Renfro, M.S., Assistant Prevention Director, University of Memphis; the middle school coordinators; and the project director.

Nancy Hepler, Ph.D, has 25 years experience developing and conducting outcome evaluations. She directs a National Institute of Justice funded research study of the success of juvenile court truancy reduction programs in Nashville and the valuations of the HUD funded Public Housing Elimination Programs administered by Nashville's Metropolitan Development and Housing Agency, and the Sumner County Middle School Coordinators grant. Dr. Hepler has directed many federal, state, and locally funded evaluation studies of alcohol and drug prevention and treatment programs funded by the Tennessee Department of Health including the governor's Prevention Initiative Evaluation of the Office of Minority Health Programs for African American Males and Females. She was a Senior Research Associate with Educational Testing Service where she worked on numerous testing and evaluation projects, including providing technical assistance to states in the evaluation of their Chapter 1 programs. As a consultant, Dr. Hepler has provided assistance in the design and implementations of evaluations to state agencies and to local programs in many states. She is experienced with providing prompt quarterly reports as well as annual reports for federally funded programs and has experience writing chapters in publications that disseminate the methodology and the findings of studies like the one proposed.

Jean Renfro, M.A., serves as Associate Project for Prevention Evaluation in the Department of Anthropology, University of Memphis. She oversees local evaluations for state-funded alcohol and drug prevention programs and provides technical assistance and training. Ms. Renfro has been in the alcohol and other drug field for more than 23 years. She works primarily in the areas of prevention and intervention, evaluating programs and services, writing grants.

References: Kim, S. (1981). Student Attitudinal Inventory of Outcome Evaluation for Adolescent Drug Abuse Prevention Programs. Journal of Primary Prevention, 2(2), Winter, 91-100. Kim, S., Crutchfield, C., Williams, C., & Hepler, N. (1994). Innovative and Unconventional Approaches to Program Evaluation in the Field of Substance Abuse Prevention: Threshold-Gating Approach Using Single System Evaluation Designs in Shakeh Jackie Katerian and William B. Hansen (Eds.) Monograph Series CSAP Special Issue: Community Partnership Program, Center for Substance Abuse Prevention, Journal of Community Psychology, 61-78.

Kim S., Kibel, B., Williams, C., & Hepler, N. (1994). Evaluating the success of community-based ATOD prevention efforts: Blending old and new approaches and methods, in CSAP Cultural Competence Monograph Series: Advance Methodological Issues in Cultural Evaluation, 4:1-17.

BUDGET

BUDGET NARRATIVE

Costs projected in the budget are reasonable, cost effective, and adequate given the services the program proposes to provide to 550 students and adults at three sites in Sumner County. The reader should note that in-kind contributions amount to at least 46% of the budget. Salaries and wages are comparable to others in similar positions within our school system. Contractual agreements will be made with the following organizations for specified services: Global Education Center will provide multicultural education; the Gallatin Civic Center will provide swimming, physical conditioning, and basketball; the Steeple Players will offer drama classes; and Dr. Nancy Hepler and Associates will provide the necessary external evaluation. Indirect costs are calculated at the standard rate of 1.65%. In year one there is a one time cost for the purchase of the Accelerated Math Program for each school site. Aside from this one time expenditure, the two following years remain basically the same. The support provided by the community partners is detailed in the Letters of Commitment (Appendix A). The following budget summaries for each of the three grant years includes in-kind funding from these partners.

U.S. DEPARTMENT OF EDUCATION

BUDGET INFORMATION

NON-CONSTRUCTION PROGRAMS

Applicants requesting funding for only one year should complete the column under "Project Year.1." Applicants requesting funding for multi-year grants should complete all applicable columns. Please read all instructions before completing form.

Name of Institution/Organization

Sumner County Board of Education

SECTION A - BUDGET SUMMARY
U.S. DEPARTMENT OF EDUCATION FUNDS

Budget Categories	Project Year 1 (a)	Project Year 2 (b)	Project Year 3 (c)	Project Year 4 (d)	Project Year 5 (e)	Total (f)
1. Personnel	197,465.00	199,337.00	201,284.00			
2. Fringe Benefits	25,907.00	26,153.00	26,408.00			
3. Travel	60,244.00	60,244.00	60,244.00			
4. Equipment						
5. Supplies	12,000.00	12,000.00	15,000.00			
6. Contractual	33,160.00	33,160.00	33,160.00			
7. Construction						
8. Other	54,905.00	48,519.00	34,919.00			
9. Total Direct Costs (lines 1-8)	383,681.00	379,413.00	371,015.00			
10. Indirect Costs	6,331.00	6,260.00	6,122.00			
11. Training Stipends						
12. Total Costs (lines 9-11)	390,012.00	385,673.00	377,137.00			

ED Form No. 524

Name of Institution/Organization

Sumner County Board of Education

Applicants requesting funding for only one year should complete the column under "Project Year 1." Applicants requesting funding for multi-year grants should complete all applicable columns. Please read all instructions before completing form.

SECTION B - BUDGET SUMMARY
NON-FEDERAL FUNDS

Budget Categories	Project Year 1 (a)	Project Year 2 (b)	Project Year 3 (c)	Project Year 4 (d)	Project Year 5 (e)	Total (f)
1. Personnel	37,635.00	37,635.00	37,635.00			
2. Fringe Benefits	4,938.00	4,938.00	4,938.00			
3. Travel						
4. Equipment						
5. Supplies	8,000.00	8,000.00	8,000.00			
6. Contractual	124,450.00	124,450.00	124,450.00			
7. Construction						
8. Other						
9. Total Direct Costs (lines 1-8)	175,023.00	175,023.00	175,023.00			
10. Indirect Costs	2,888.00	2,888.00	2,888.00			
11. Training Stipends						
12. Total Costs (lines 9-11)	177,911.00	177,911.00	177,911.00			

SECTION C - OTHER BUDGET INFORMATION (see instructions)

ED Form No. 524

UNITY.COM COMMUNITY LEARNING CENTER BUDGET: YEAR 1

BUDGET	EXPLANATION	USDE	IN KIND
Personnel			
Personnel CurriculumCoordinator	$90/wk x 39wks		$3,510
Safe & Drug Free Coordinator	$75/wk 39wks		$2,925
Project Director	11 months certified administrator	$46,805	
Site Manager (3)	3 x $15.00 x 4 hr/day x 180 days	$32,400	
Lead Teachers (3)	3 x $20/hr x 3 hrs/day x 180days certified teachers	$32,400	
Related Arts Teachers (3)	3 x$20/hr x 3hrs/day x 180 days	$32,400	
Community Teachers (6)	6 x $8/hr x 3hrs x 180days	$25,920	
Counselor (3)	3 x $20/hr x 6hr/wk x 36/wks certified counselor	$12,960	
Technical Specialist (1)	$20/hr x 9hr/wk x 36 certified	$6,480	
Librarian	$15 x 15 hrs/wk x 36wks	$8,100	
Total Personnel		**$197,465**	**$37,635**
Fringe	13.12%	**$25,907**	**$4,938**
Travel: Project Dir. Meeting	1 meeting x 2 people at $1,000	$2,000	
Professional Development	1 trip x 3 people x $750	$2,250	
Bus Transportation (3)	personnel $12/hr x 20hr/wk x 36 wks	$25,920	
Mileage	1.25/mile x 200miles/wk x 36 wks	$27,000	
Family Field Trips	3 Buses x 2 trips	$1,008	
	Gas	$2,066	
Total Travel		**$60,244**	
Supplies	General/ recreational supplies/	**$12,00**	
	350 x $20.00 registration fee/scholarships available		**$8,000**
Contractual: Global Education	Cultural Drum Corp & Dance Training/Therapeutic Writing Expression	$6,000	
Gallatin Civic Center	2 junior lifeguard instructors 2 x $7/hr x 3 hr/day x 180 days	$7,560	
	$2 per student x 100 x 180 days use of pool, weight room, courts		$36,000
Evaluation	Dr. N. Hepler & Associates/University of Memphis	$18,600	$9,000
Strengthening Families	Family substance abuse program 3 sites 11 week program/3 monthly		$9,000
YMCA	Leadership ; environmental; 36wks		$2,000
Girl Scouts	Hispanic - group mentoring		$6,800
Steeple Players	Drama club x 36 wks	$1,000	$2,500
Gallatin Arts Council	City murals & family arts x 36 wks		$4,000
Adult Education	GED preparation & adult education x 36 wks		$26,600
STAR	Truancy reduction class x 36 wks		$7,000
Gallatin Health Dept.	Health risk assessments, personnel training, health education x 36wks		$13,750
Volunteer State College	Tutor, mentor Training, radio station facility		$6,800
Alcohol & Drug Council of Middle TN	Alcohol and drug training		$1,000
Total Contractual		**$33,160**	**$124,450**
Other: Field Trip	Chattanooga Aquarium 120 students x $8.95 120 adults x $14.54	$2,819	
After School Snacks	150 x .50/day x 180 days (to be supplemented/reimbursed USDA)	$13,500	
Technology	Accelerated math program - $862 x 3 sites - one time cost	$26,586	
Communication	printing, postage, and telephone x 3	$7,500	
Training	Violence prevention, technology training	$4,500	
Total Other		**$54,905**	**$175,023**
Total Direct Cost		**$383,681**	
Indirect Cost	indirect cost 1.65%	**$6,331**	**$2,790**
Total Costs		**$390,012**	**$177,911**

UNITY.COM COMMUNITY LEARNING CENTER BUDGET: YEAR 2

BUDGET	EXPLANATION	USDE	IN KIND
Personnel Curriculum Coordinator	$90/wk x 39wks		$3,510
Safe & Drug Free Coordinator	$75/wk 39wks		$2,925
Project Director	11 months certified administrator x 4% raise	$48,677	
Site Manager (3)	3 x $15.00 x 4 hr/day x 180 days	$32,400	
Lead Teachers (3)	3 x $20/hr x 3 hrs/day x 180days certified teachers	$32,400	
Related Arts Teachers (3)	3 x$20/hr x 3hrs/day x 180 days	$32,400	
Community Teachers (6)	6 x $8/hr x 3hrs x 180days	$25,920	
Counselor (3)	3 x $20/hr x 6hr/wk x 36/wks certified counselor	$12,960	
Technical Specialist (1)	$20/hr x 9hr/wk x 36 certified	$6,480	
Librarian	$15 x 15 hrs/wk x 36wks	$8,100	
Total Personnel		$199,337	$37,635
Fringe	13.12%	$26,153	$4,938
Travel: Project Dir. Meeting	1 meeting x 2 people at $1,000	$2,000	
Professional Development	1 trip x 3 people x $750	$2,250	
Bus Transportation (3)	personnel $12/hr x 20hr/wk x 36 wks	$25,920	
Mileage	1.25/mile x 200miles/wk x 36 wks	$27,000	
Family Field Trips	3 Buses x 2 trips	$1,008	
	Gas	$2,066	
Total Travel		$60,244	
Supplies	General/ recreational supplies/	$12,000	
	350 x $20.00 registration fee/scholarships available		$8,000
Contractual: Global Education Ctr.	Cultural Drum Corp & Dance Training/Therapeutic Writing Expression	$6,000	
Gallatin Civic Center	2 junior lifeguard instructors 2 x $7/hr x 3 hr/day x 180 days	$7,560	
	$2 per student x 100 x 180 days use of pool, weight room, courts		$36,000
Evaluation	Dr. N. Hepler & Associates/University of Memphis	$18,600	$9,000
Strengthening Families	Family substance abuse program 3 sites 11 week program/3 monthly		$9,000
YMCA	Leadership ; environmental; 36wks		$2,000
Girl Scouts	Hispanic - group mentoring		$6,800
Steeple Players	Drama club x 36 wks	$1,000	$2,500
Gallatin Arts Council	City murals & family arts x 36 wks		$4,000
Adult Education	GED preparation & adult education x 36 wks		$26,600
STAR	Truancy reduction class x 36 wks		$7,000
Gallatin Health Dept.	Health risk assessments, personnel training, health education x 36wks		$13,750
Volunteer State College	Tutor, mentor Training, radio station facility		$6,800
Alcohol & Drug Council of Middle TN	Alcohol and drug training		$1,000
Total Contractual		$33,160	$124,450
Other : Field Trip	Kentucky Caves 120 students x $8.95 120 adults x $14.54	$2,819	
After School Snacks	150 x .50/day x 180 days (to be supplemented/reimbursed USDA)	$13,500	
Training	Continued education for instructors	$4,500	
Computers	1 computer x 3 sites	$4,600	
Art Education	pottery kiln $1,000 x 3 sites	$3,000	
Technology	Software licenses (6 x $1,100)	$6,600	
Gems Series:	Bubbleology, Math World, Crime Lab Chemistry Kits $2,000 x 3	$6,000	
Communication	printing, postage, and telephone x 3	$7,500	
Total Other		$48,519	
Total Direct Cost		$379,413	$175,023
Indirect Cost	indirect cost 1.65%	$6,260	$2,888
Total Costs		$385,673	$177,911

UNITY.COM COMMUNITY LEARNING CENTER BUDGET: YEAR 3

BUDGET	EXPLANATION	USDE	IN KIND
Personnel			
Personnel CurriculumCoordinator	$90/wk x 39wks		$3,510
Safe & Drug Free Coordinator	$75/wk 39wks		$2,925
Project Director	11 months certified administrator	$46,805	
Site Manager (3)	3 x $15.00 x 4 hr/day x 180 days	$32,400	
Lead Teachers (3)	3 x $20/hr x 3 hrs/day x 180days certified teachers	$32,400	
Related Arts Teachers (3)	3 x$20/hr x 3hrs/day x 180 days	$32,400	
Community Teachers (6)	6 x $8/hr x 3hrs x 180days	$25,920	
Counselor (3)	3 x $20/hr x 6hr/wk x 36/wks certified counselor	$12,960	
Technical Specialist (1)	$20/hr x 9hr/wk x 36 certified	$6,480	
Librarian	$15 x 15 hrs/wk x 36wks	$8,100	
Total Personnel		**$197,465**	**$37,635**
Fringe	13.12%	**$25,907**	**$4,938**
Travel: Project Dir. Meeting	1 meeting x 2 people at $1,000	$2,000	
Professional Development	1 trip x 3 people x $750	$2,250	
Bus Transportation (3)	personnel $12/hr x 20hr/wk x 36 wks	$25,920	
Mileage	1.25/mile x 200miles/wk x 36 wks	$27,000	
Family Field Trips	3 Buses x 2 trips	$1,008	
	Gas	$2,066	
Total Travel		**$60,244**	
Supplies	General/ recreational supplies/	**$12,00**	
	350 x $20.00 registration fee/scholarships available		**$8,000**
Contractual: Global Education	Cultural Drum Corp & Dance Training/Therapeutic Writing Expression	$6,000	
Gallatin Civic Center	2 junior lifeguard instructors 2 x $7/hr x 3 hr/day x 180 days	$7,560	
	$2 per student x 100 x 180 days use of pool, weight room, courts		$36,000
Evaluation	Dr. N. Hepler & Associates/University of Memphis	$18,600	$9,000
Strengthening Families	Family substance abuse program 3 sites 11 week program/3 monthly		$9,000
YMCA	Leadership ; environmental; 36wks		$2,000
Girl Scouts	Hispanic - group mentoring		$6,800
Steeple Players	Drama club x 36 wks	$1,000	$2,500
Art Resources of TN - Sumner ARTS	Character Education murals at schools & family arts x 36 wks		$4,000
Adult Education	GED preparation & adult education x 36 wks		$26,600
STAR	Truancy reduction class x 36 wks		$7,000
Gallatin Health Dept.	Health risk assessments, personnel training, health education x 36wks		$13,750
Volunteer State College	Tutor, mentor Training, radio station facility		$6,800
Alcohol & Drug Council of Middle TN	Alcohol and drug training		$1,000
Total Contractual		**$33,160**	**$124,450**
Other : Field Trip	Chattanooga Aquarium 120 students x $8.95 120 adults x $14.54	$2,819	
After School Snacks	150 x .50/day x 180 days (to be supplemented/reimbursed USDA)	$13,500	
Technology	Accelerated math program - $862 x 3 sites - one time cost	$26,586	
Communication	printing, postage, and telephone x 3	$7,500	
Training	Violence prevention, technology training	$4,500	
Total Other		**$54,905**	**$175,023**
Total Direct Cost		**$383,681**	
Indirect Cost	indirect cost 1.65%	**$6,331**	**$2,790**
Total Costs		**$390,012**	**$177,911**

8

Implementing a Fundraising Plan for Your School or School District

In this chapter you will:

❑ Understand that school districts are employing full-time staff and consultants, as needed, for their development offices

❑ Identify reasons for hiring full-time staff and consultants

❑ Identify where to look for staff and consultants

❑ Become familiar with an implementation plan utilizing consultants and full-time staff members

Because needs and opportunities are so great, many school districts are moving in the direction of hiring full-time staff members and consultants to assist them in establishing a development office. Depending on the size of the district and available financial resources, full-time staff might include an executive director of the school or district foundation, assistants as appropriate, office space, secretarial staff, and a number of full-time grant writers and specialists. It is recommended that consultants be employed, as needed, to work with full-time staff and provide expertise and staff development. This allows the school district flexibility in selecting specific people for specific tasks, and also does not obligate the district to long-term contracts or fringe benefits. Consultants are generally independent contractors who sign a contract with the district to complete a specific task by a specific date for a specific consultant fee. Consultants are basically in business for themselves and are responsible for their own benefits, office space, and secretarial services, unless other arrangements have been made.

In selecting staff for your school or school district, it is important to understand that in most instances, public school people have more experience in obtaining government grants than they have in obtaining corporate and foundation grants as well as grants and gifts from individuals. While this book will do much to assist teachers, principals, parents, the superintendent, and others in "gearing up" their fundraising efforts, it is recommended that until such time as full-time staff is employed and trained, consultants be hired to assist the schools in areas of need to enable them to become competitive as they seek their fair share of the fundraising pie.

A good place to find full-time, qualified staff for your development office is by placing an announcement in the *Chronicle of Philanthropy* (Tel. 202-466-1230). Reading the *Chronicle* will also assist you in identifying consultants and consultant companies. Going onto its website at *http://www.philanthropy.com* is also recommend to familiarize yourself with the enormity of the fundraising field. Be selective in choosing staff and consultants to assist you in organizing your development office and in obtaining grants and gifts. There are many good people and companies out there who can help. For example, if you are thinking about hiring staff for your development office, why not take a look at private K-12 schools? They have been raising millions of dollars for years and have people on staff with areas of expertise that you might be looking for.

As far as consultants are concerned, take a look at their recent track records. Ask about their experience at the elementary and secondary school levels. Check their references to find out if they are able to work cooperatively with teachers, principals, parents, volunteers, and others. Finally, inquire about their fee schedules. Most consultants will charge you a daily rate and multiply that rate by the number of days they estimate it will take them to complete a project. Be wary of consultants who will propose to work for you for no fee up front but on a percentage basis. These are consultants who are usually just getting started and are attempting to get their foot in the door. To get a contract, they will make this kind of proposal. This arrangement is not recommended, even though it sounds enticing. For example: If the consultant was working on 15% of gross for a winning grant that comes in at $1 million, are you prepared to justify to your community paying the consultant $150,000 for one grant? Also, which category of the budget would this fee come out of and would it be legal to do this in your state?

One of the great things about hiring full-time staff and consultants, as needed, is that the development office, with reasonable expectations and adequate time, will become a *profit center* for your school or school district. These will probably be the only positions in the schools that bring in more money then go out. Below you will find some reasons for hiring full-time staff and also utilizing the services of fundraising consultants in the schools.

Some Reasons for Hiring Full-Time Staff and Consultants as Needed in the Schools

A qualified full-time staff member or a fundraising consultant should:

■ Have full-time fundraising experience at the K-12 level.

■ Know how to obtain corporate, foundation, and government grants as well as grants and gifts from individuals.

■ Know how to do prospect research and respond to Requests for Proposals (RFPs).

■ Know how to match up school district needs with corporate, foundation, and government interests and funding levels.

■ Understand the importance of getting to know many of the wealthy people in the community who give to good causes and know ways of soliciting monies from these individuals.

■ Know how to conduct and manage an annual and capital campaign, and understand what planned giving is and how to implement a planned giving program.

■ Know how to work cooperatively with district-level administrators, principals, evaluators, teachers, parents, and community leaders.

■ Relate well to program officers and chief executive officers of funding agencies and understand the nurturing process that takes place before a grant is awarded.

■ Be articulate and knowledgeable of education issues and needs from pre-kindergarten through grade 12.

■ Set a good example for the grant writing team by being a successful grant writer, being well organized and articulate, making good use of technology, and meeting all deadlines.

■ Have established a successful track record of assisting schools and school districts in obtaining funding on a continuing basis and be called upon to teach others how to do it.

■ After a realistic period of time, become a profit center for the school or school district.

I have introduced and used the following plan, called **Implementing a Fundraising Plan Utilizing Consultants or Full-time Staff Member(s)**, as a consultant in a number of school districts across the country. If your school or school district employs full-time staff for fundraising purposes, you can substitute the word "full-time staff" for "consultant" or use a combination of the two.

IMPLEMENTING A FUNDRAISING PLAN UTILIZING CONSULTANTS OR FULL-TIME STAFF MEMBER(S)

1.0 Mission Statement: To work cooperatively with the Board of Trustees, the Superintendent, the Staff, the Parents, the Community, and others in soliciting external funding for the school district from Corporations, Foundations, the Government, and Individuals.

2.0 Consultant assists the district in identifying and prioritizing most urgent fundraising needs including cost projections and time projections.

3.0 Consultant researches and identifies possible corporate, foundation, government, and individual grant opportunities based upon needs identified in 2.0.

4.0 Consultant recommends to the school district the funding sources to pursue based upon research conducted and possibilities for approval. Consultant obtains grant applications.

5.0 Consultant works with school site principals, teachers, curriculum specialists, parents, institutions of higher education, and others in gathering the needed data and support for submission of grant proposals.

6.0 Consultant edits the data, places the information in proper format, prepares grant proposal, gets needed approvals and signatures, and submits to funding source by deadline date.

7.0 Consultant establishes a funding resource library, assists school sites in responding to requests for proposals (RFPs), and trains teachers, administrators, and others in fundraising, as needed.

Assignment

Implementing a Fundraising Plan for Your School or School District

1. Obtain a copy of the *Chronicle of Philanthropy* and familiarize yourself with it.
2. Read the Employment Opportunities section and attempt to locate an advertisement for a K-12 position. Study the specifications for the position.
3. Design your own specifications for the following positions and prepare them for distribution and discussion:
   a. Executive Director of School (District) Foundation
   b. Director of Corporate, Foundation, and Government Grants
   c. Director of Individual Giving
   d. Full-Time Grantwriter

9
Conclusion

In this book, I have talked about the many fundraising opportunities available to the public schools, including government grants, corporate and foundation grants, and grants and gifts from individuals. I have discussed recent trends in giving and the coming boom in philanthropy that should have a significant impact on the public schools. I have attempted to be practical in my suggestions and approach based upon my background of experience as a classroom teacher, a grant writer, and a fundraising consultant. I have suggested new avenues of fundraising for the public schools such as individual solicitation, annual and capital campaigns, and planned giving.

A comprehensive approach to grant writing, organized into two chapters, is also included. Examples of winning proposals are included to enable you to familiarize yourself with different writing styles, requirements, content, and programs. A fundraising implementation plan is suggested and provides assistance at the school or district level related to staffing and consultant needs. The formation of a Local Education Foundation at the school or district level has also been discussed.

Most chapters include assignments that provide needed learning activities and experiences. Bibliographical citations of worthwhile books, periodicals, software, and newsletters are presented and relevant World Wide Web sites are listed. All of these resources should save you significant amounts of time in doing prospect research and further study.

After reading this book, it is my hope that you will feel more confident and knowledgeable of the fundraising field. Also, that you will become excited and optimistic about the future of fundraising and the many resources available to you. There is a lot of interest in providing financial help to the public schools. We are at the threshold of a boom in philanthropy never seen before. There are billions of dollars out there waiting to be tapped. With your help, the kids and the schools will benefit. Don't miss the chance!

Appendix 1
21st Century Community Learning Centers Program

CFDA No. 84.287
Blank Application for Grants

**U.S. Department of Education
Application Control Center
Regional Office Building 3, Room 3633
7th and D Streets, SW
Washington, D.C. 20202-4725**

21st Century Community Learning Centers Program

Application for Grants

CFDA # 84.287

Office of Elementary and Secondary Education
U.S. Department of Education
Washington, DC 20202

Fax: 202-260-3420
e-mail: 21stCCLC@ed.gov
Website: http://www.ed.gov/21stcclc

Applications Due: March 20, 2000

21st Century Community Learning Centers
Attn: CFDA No. 84.287
U.S. Department of Education
Application Control Center
Regional Office Building 3, Room 3633
7th & D Streets, SW
Washington, DC 20202-4725

Form Approved
OMB No. 1850-0711, Exp. Date 11/30/2001

21st CENTURY COMMUNITY LEARNING CENTERS PROGRAM APPLICATION FOR GRANTS

TABLE OF CONTENTS

What is the 21st Century Community Learning Centers Program?

The 21st Century Community Learning Centers Program was established by Congress to award grants to rural and inner-city public schools, or consortia of such schools, to enable them to plan, implement, or expand projects that benefit the educational, health, social services, cultural and recreational needs of the community. School-based learning centers can provide safe, drug-free, supervised and cost-effective afterschool, weekend or summer havens for children, youth and their families. Grants awarded under this program may be used to plan, implement, or expand community learning centers.

The authorizing legislation states that schools "should collaborate with other public and nonprofit agencies and organizations, local businesses, educational entities (such as vocational and adult education programs, school-to-work programs, community colleges, and universities), recreational, cultural, and other community and human service entities, for the purpose of meeting the needs of, and expanding the opportunities available to, the residents of the communities served by such schools." By statute, applications must include "a description of the collaborative efforts to be undertaken by community-based organizations, related public agencies, businesses, or other appropriate organizations."

The program is designed to target funds to high-need rural and urban communities that have low achieving students and high rates of juvenile crime, school violence, and student drug abuse, but lack the resources to establish afterschool centers.

What is the definition of a 21st Century Community Learning Center?

A Community Learning Center is an entity *within a public elementary, middle or secondary school building* that (1) provides educational, recreational, health, and social service programs for residents of all ages within a local community, and (2) is operated by a local educational agency (LEA) in conjunction with local governmental agencies, businesses, vocational education programs, institutions of higher education, community colleges, and cultural, recreational, and other community and human service entities. An LEA--usually synonymous with a school district--is an entity defined under state law as being legally responsible for providing public education to elementary and secondary students. In some states this may include an entity performing a service function for public schools, such as an intermediate service agency. The full definition of this term is set out in Section 14101(18) of the Elementary and Secondary Education Act (20 U.S.C. 8801(18)).

What are the components of a high quality community learning center?

Comprehensive Program Planning for the Integration of 21st Century Community Learning Centers with Regular Day Programs and Community Partners, a publication produced by the North Central Regional Educational Laboratory (NCREL), describes characteristics, policies, and programs to help integrate the afterschool program, the regular school day, and existing partnerships within the community. A review of the research on Community Learning Centers reveals the following 16 characteristics that lead to comprehensive program planning for integration:

related public agencies, businesses, or other appropriate organizations." For instance, community-based organizations may receive a contract from a grantee to provide after-school services at the Community Learning Center. **However, only public schools or LEAs can receive or administer a grant.**

What will be the time period, size and number of grants?

Time period. By statute, a 21st Century Community Learning Center grant cannot exceed three years.

Size of grants. By statute, the Department will not consider for funding any application that requests less than $35,000.

Note: In 1999, the average grant size was approximately $365,000 and the typical grant supported three Centers, at an average cost per Center of approximately $125,000. Annual costs per Center generally ranged from $35,000 to $200,000, depending on the number of individuals served, the array of proposed activities, and the availability of additional resources. An LEA with more than one school seeking to participate in this program is encouraged to submit a single application on their behalf, although large LEAs may consider submitting more than one application, e.g., separate applications for school clusters in different neighborhoods.

Number of grants. The amount of available funds in FY 2000 for new awards under this Program is approximately $185 million. It is estimated that 350-500 new grants supporting a total of approximately 1500 Centers will be awarded. However, the actual number of grants and Centers will depend upon the characteristics of the programs described in the highest-rated applications.

What regulations apply to this program?

The following regulations are applicable to the 21st Century Community Learning Centers Program: (a) The Education Department General Administrative Regulations (EDGAR) in 34 CFR Parts 75, 77, 79, 80, 81, 82, 85, and 86, and (b) 34 CFR Part 299.

What kinds of program activities are required?

To receive a grant under this program, applicants must provide services that address the absolute priority and must address at least four of the program activities stated in the law, as described below:

Absolute Priority: We will fund <u>only</u> those applications for 21st Century Community Learning Centers grants that include, among the array of services required and authorized by the statute, *activities that offer significant expanded learning opportunities for children and youth in the community and that contribute to reduced drug use and violence.*

Program Activities: (1) Literacy education programs; (2) Senior citizen programs; (3) Children's day care services; (4) Integrated education, health, social service, recreational, or cultural programs; (5) Summer and weekend school programs in conjunction with recreation competition. The peer reviewers of your proposal will use these criteria to guide their reviews, so it is in your interest to be familiar with them.

(1)   Need for project. (30 points)

(A) **The extent to which the proposed project will provide services or otherwise address the needs of students at risk of educational failure.**

Suggestions/Guidance for applicants: It is recommended that you describe how the services that you are proposing will help meet the needs of the community by citing the factors that place students at risk of educational failure. These factors may include the poverty rates in the communities to be served, the percentage and/or rapid growth of limited English proficient students and adults, the percentage of Title I students, the dropout rates, and the literacy rates and education levels in the community. We suggest that you use specific and relevant data regarding the students and community members to be served by the project and the needs of the community. Applicants are advised that a needs inventory may be helpful in determining the needs of the community and the gaps in the services that are available. The services to be provided should be closely tied to the identified needs.

(2)   Quality of project design. (30 points)

(A) **The extent to which the goals, objectives, and outcomes to be achieved by the proposed project are clearly specified and measurable.**

(B) **The extent to which the design of the proposed project is appropriate to, and will successfully address, the needs of the target population or other identified needs.**

(C) **The extent to which the proposed project will establish linkages with other appropriate agencies and organizations providing services to the target population.**

Suggestions/Guidance for applicants: We recommend that you provide a clear description of the activities to be provided by the project and the roles to be played by each of the partners, who will do what, when, and where, to what ends, and with what anticipated results. It is also suggested that you carefully design your activities to address the central causes of the needs you described and the desired outcomes. Providing measurable goals, objectives and outcomes for the project may be helpful as well.

In addition, we suggest that you describe how all consortium members are active players devoting both the time and resources to plan and implement the project. Please include letters of commitment and support demonstrating buy-in from senior administrators of partnering organizations in the appendix. Applicants are advised that the quality of letters of support, with a clear representation of the partner's continuing responsibilities, is more important than the quantity.

(3)   Adequacy of resources. (15 points)

(A) **The adequacy of support, including facilities, equipment, supplies, and other resources, from the applicant organization or the lead applicant organization.**

(B) **The extent to which the costs are reasonable in relation to the number of persons to be served and to the anticipated results and benefits.**

indicating: (1) what types of data will be collected; (2) when various types of data will be collected; (3) what designs and methods will be used; (4) what instruments will be developed and when; (5) how the data will be analyzed; (6) when reports of results and outcomes will become available; and (7) how information will be used by the project to monitor progress and to provide accountability information to stakeholders about success at the project site(s). Note: The performance indicators may be found in the appendix of this application package.

<u>**Competitive Priority 1.**</u> **(5 points)**
Projects designed to assist students to meet or exceed state and local standards in core academic subjects such as reading, mathematics or science, as appropriate to the needs of the participating children.

> *Note: It is our experience that successful applicants address the needs of potential dropouts and students otherwise at risk of academic failure, including students living in poverty and students with limited English proficiency.*

What is the Government Performance and Results Act?

The Government Performance and Results Act (GPRA) of 1993 places new management requirements on Federal agencies, which must describe the goals and objectives of their programs, identify resources and actions needed to accomplish these goals and objectives, develop a means of measuring progress made, and regularly report on their achievement. One important source of program information on successes and lessons learned is the project evaluation conducted under individual grants.

The goal of the 21st Century Community Learning Centers Program is to enable rural and inner-city public elementary and secondary schools, or consortia or such schools, to plan, implement, or expand projects that benefit the educational, health, social service, cultural, and recreational needs of their communities. **The objectives for the Program's projects, along with the performance indicators established to measure the Program's effectiveness in meeting its goals, are included in the appendix to this application package.** Projects are required to submit data on relevant performance indicators as part of their annual and final performance reports to the U.S. Department of Education. The performance report forms are available on the program Website. Projects are also required to participate in any national evaluations that the Department may conduct of the Program.

How do I prepare an application for a 21st Century Community Learning Centers Grant?

Carefully read the entire application package before beginning to prepare an application. The application package clearly identifies who is eligible to apply under this competition, what applicants must propose to do, what must be contained in an application, and what criteria will be used to evaluate applications. Copies of the authorizing statute as well as supplementary materials describing the components of high-quality after-school programs and Community Learning Centers are provided in the Appendix to this application package.

b. <u>Evidence of previous success</u>. Include a brief summary of any evaluation studies, reports, or research that may document the effectiveness or success of the consortium or the activities/services proposed in the narrative section of the application.

c. <u>Equitable Access and Participation</u>. Section 427 requires every applicant (other than an individual person) to include in its application a description of the steps the applicant proposes to ensure **equitable access** to, and participation in, its Federally-assisted program for students, teachers, and other program beneficiaries with special needs. Detailed instructions about how an applicant may comply with these requirements are provided in the Appendix to this application package.

Other attachments to the application are strongly discouraged! Reviewers will have a limited time to read each application, and their consideration of the application against the selection criteria will be limited to the sections of the application and the appendix listed above. Supplementary materials such as videotapes, CD-ROMs, files on disks, commercial publications, press clippings, testimonial letters, etc., will not be reviewed nor will they be returned to the applicant.

How do I submit an application?

The deadline for transmitting applications is **March 20, 2000**. All applications must be **postmarked on or before** that date. This closing date and procedures for guaranteeing timely submission will be strictly observed. No supplemental or revised information from applicants will be accepted after the closing date, or after an application has been submitted. Applications delivered by hand before the deadline date will be accepted daily between the hours of 8:00 a.m. and 4:00 p.m., Eastern Time, except Saturdays, Sundays and Federal holidays.

All applicants are encouraged to submit one signed original and four additional copies of the entire application, beginning with the Cover Page. Applicants are also encouraged to submit all copies of the application together in one package, to ensure that the Application Control Center does not log in the same application more than once.

Applications submitted by mail should be sent to the following address:

21st Century Community Learning Centers
Attn: CFDA No. 84.287
U.S. Department of Education
Application Control Center
Regional Office Building 3, Room 3633
7th & D Streets, SW
Washington, DC 20202-4725

(Note: the telephone number for the Application Control Center is 202-708-8493)

<u>To prove that an application was transmitted in a timely manner, an application must show proof of mailing consisting of one of the following:</u>

The Department provides information about grants and contract opportunities electronically in several ways:

ED Internet Home Page	http://www.ed.gov/GrantApps/	(WWW address)
	gopher://gopher.ed.gov	(Gopher address)
Office of the Chief	http://ocfo.ed.gov	(WWW address)
Financial Officer (OCFO)	http://gcs.ed.gov	(WWW address)

Information about the Department's funding opportunities, including copies of application notices for other discretionary grant competitions, can also be viewed on the Department's electronic bulletin board (connect by modem to 202-260-9950). However, the official application notice for a discretionary grant competition is the notice published in the *Federal Register.*

Required Forms

ED Form 424 and instructions

Program Summary and Abstract

ED Form 524 and instructions

Assurances - Non-Construction Programs

Certification Regarding Lobbying, Debarment, Suspension, and Other Responsibility Matters; Drug-Free Workplace Requirements

Certification Regarding Debarment, Suspension, Ineligibility and Voluntary Exclusion Lower Tier Covered Transactions

Disclosure of Lobbying Activities

Intergovernmental Review--Executive Order 12372

Application for Federal Education Assistance

Note: If available, please provide application package on diskette and specify the file format.

U.S. Department of Education

Form Approved
OMB No. 1875-0106
Exp. 06/30/2001

Applicant Information

1. Name and Address

Legal Name:_____

Address:_____

_____

_____

City _____ State _____ County _____ ZIP Code + 4 _____

Organizational Unit

2. Applicant's D-U-N-S Number ☐☐☐☐☐☐☐☐☐

3. Applicant's T-I-N ☐☐ - ☐☐☐☐☐☐☐

4. Catalog of Federal Domestic Assistance #: **8 4** ° ☐☐☐ ➡ Title:_____

5. Project Director:_____

Address:_____

_____

City _____ State _____ ZIP Code + 4 _____

Tel. #: ( ) _____ - _____   Fax #: ( ) _____ - _____

E-Mail Address:_____

6. Is the applicant delinquent on any Federal debt? ☐ Yes ☐ No

(If "Yes," attach an explanation.)

7. Type of Applicant *(Enter appropriate letter in the box.)* ☐

A State
B County
C Municipal
D Township
E Interstate
F Intermunicipal
G Special District

H Independent School District
I Public College or University
J Private, Non-Profit College or University
K Indian Tribe
L Individual
M Private, Profit-Making Organization
N Other *(Specify):*_____

8. Novice Applicant ☐ Yes ☐ No

Application Information

9. Type of Submission:

—PreApplication
☐ Construction
☐ Non-Construction

—Application
☐ Construction
☐ Non-Construction

10. Is application subject to review by Executive Order 12372 process?

☐ Yes *(Date made available to the Executive Order 12372 process for review):* ____/____/_____

☐ No *(If "No," check appropriate box below.)*
☐ Program is not covered by E.O. 12372.
☐ Program has not been selected by State for review.

11. Proposed Project Dates:

Start Date: ____/____/_____   **End Date:** ____/____/_____

12. Are any research activities involving human subjects planned at any time during the proposed project period? ☐ Yes ☐ No

a. If "Yes," Exemption(s) #:

b. Assurance of Compliance #:

OR

c. IRB approval date: _____
{ ☐ Full IRB **or**
☐ Expedited Review

13. Descriptive Title of Applicant's Project:

Estimated Funding

14a. Federal	$	.00
b. Applicant	$	.00
c. State	$	.00
d. Local	$	.00
e. Other	$	.00
f. Program Income	$	.00
g. TOTAL	$_____	.00

Authorized Representative Information

15. To the best of my knowledge and belief, all data in this preapplication/application are true and correct. The document has been duly authorized by the governing body of the applicant and the applicant will comply with the attached assurances if the assistance is awarded.

a. Typed Name of Authorized Representative

b. Title

c. Tel. #: ( ) _____ - _____   Fax #: ( ) _____ - _____

d. E-Mail Address:

e. **Signature of Authorized Representative**   Date:____/____/_____

REV. 11/12/99

ED 424

PROGRAM SUMMARY AND ABSTRACT

Name and address of applicant:

Contact information:
Name:
Title:
Phone: Fax:
e-mail:

District Common Core of Data Number:

Program title:

This program will serve (insert number): _____ rural public schools _____ inner city public schools

The applicant intends to provide services within the following Empowerment Zone or Enterprise Community (identify if applicable):

Please provide the name of each school that will have a Community Learning Center:

In the schools to be served (please provide the totals for all schools):
Number of students served _____ Community members served _____ Grade levels served _____
Students who are: eligible for free or reduced-price lunch _____ % Limited English proficient _____ %

Program Abstract (single-spaced on remainder of page)

U.S. DEPARTMENT OF EDUCATION

BUDGET INFORMATION

NON-CONSTRUCTION PROGRAMS

OMB Control Number: 1890-0004

Expiration Date: 02/28/2003

Name of Institution/Organization

Applicants requesting funding for only one year should complete the column under "Project Year 1." Applicants requesting funding for multi-year grants should complete all applicable columns. Please read all instructions before completing form.

SECTION A - BUDGET SUMMARY
U.S. DEPARTMENT OF EDUCATION FUNDS

Budget Categories	Project Year 1 (a)	Project Year 2 (b)	Project Year 3 (c)	Project Year 4 (d)	Project Year 5 (e)	Total (f)
1. Personnel						
2. Fringe Benefits						
3. Travel						
4. Equipment						
5. Supplies						
6. Contractual						
7. Construction						
8. Other						
9. Total Direct Costs (lines 1-8)						
10. Indirect Costs						
11. Training Stipends						
12. Total Costs (lines 9-11)						

ED Form No. 524

Public reporting burden for this collection of information is estimated to vary from 13 to 22 hours per response, with an average of 17.5 hours per response, including the time reviewing instructions, searching existing data sources, gathering and maintaining the data needed, and completing and reviewing the collection of information. Send comments regarding this burden estimate or any other aspect of this collection of information, including suggestions for reducing this burden, to the U.S. Department of Education, Information Management and Compliance Division, Washington, D.C. 20202-4651; and the Office of Management and Budget, Paperwork Reduction Project 1875-0102, Washington DC 20503.

INSTRUCTIONS FOR ED FORM 524

General Instructions

This form is used to apply to individual U.S. Department of Education discretionary grant programs. Unless directed otherwise, provide the same budget information for each year of the multi-year funding request. Pay attention to applicable program specific instructions, if attached.

Section A - Budget Summary
U.S. Department of Education Funds

All applicants must complete Section A and provide a breakdown by the applicable budget categories shown in lines 1-11.

Lines 1-11, columns (a)-(e): For each project year for which funding is requested, show the total amount requested for each applicable budget category.

Lines 1-11, column (f): Show the multi-year total for each budget category. If funding is requested for only one project year, leave this column blank.

Line 12, columns (a)-(e): Show the total budget request for each project year for which funding is requested.

Line 12, column (f): Show the total amount requested for all project years. If funding is requested for only one year, leave this space blank.

Section B - Budget Summary
Non-Federal Funds

If you are required to provide or volunteer to provide matching funds or other non-Federal resources to the project, these should be shown for each applicable budget category on lines 1-11 of Section B.

Lines 1-11, columns (a)-(e): For each project year for which matching funds or other contributions are provided, show the total

contribution for each applicable budget category.

Lines 1-11, column (f): Show the multi-year total for each budget category. If non-Federal contributions are provided for only one year, leave this column blank.

Line 12, columns (a)-(e): Show the total matching or other contribution for each project year.

Line 12, column (f): Show the total amount to be contributed for all years of the multi-year project. If non-Federal contributions are provided for only one year, leave this space blank.

Section C - Other Budget Information
Pay attention to applicable program specific instructions, if attached.

1. Provide an itemized budget breakdown, by project year, for each budget category listed in Sections A and B.

2. If applicable to this program, enter the type of indirect rate (provisional, predetermined, final or fixed) that will be in effect during the funding period. In addition, enter the estimated amount of the base to which the rate is applied, and the total indirect expense.

3. If applicable to this program, provide the rate and base on which fringe benefits are calculated.

4. Provide other explanations or comments you deem necessary.

OMB Approval No. 0348-0040

ASSURANCES - NON-CONSTRUCTION PROGRAMS

Public reporting burden for this collection of information is estimated to average 15 minutes per response, including time for reviewing instructions, searching existing data sources, gathering and maintaining the data needed, and completing and reviewing the collection of information. Send comments regarding the burden estimate or any other aspect of this collection of information, including suggestions for reducing this burden, to the Office of Management and Budget, Paperwork Reduction Project (0348-0040), Washington, DC 20503

PLEASE DO NOT RETURN YOUR COMPLETED FORM TO THE OFFICE OF MANAGEMENT AND BUDGET. SEND IT TO THE ADDRESS PROVIDED BY THE SPONSORING AGENCY.

Note: Certain of these assurances may not be applicable to your project or program. If you have questions, please contact the awarding agency. Further, certain Federal awarding agencies may require applicants to certify to additional assurances. If such is the case, you will be notified.

As the duly authorized representative of the applicant I certify that the applicant:

1. Has the legal authority to apply for Federal assistance, and the institutional, managerial and financial capability (including funds sufficient to pay the non-Federal share of project cost) to ensure proper planning, management, and completion of the project described in this application.

2. Will give the awarding agency, the Comptroller General of the United States, and if appropriate, the State, through any authorized representative, access to and the right to examine all records, books, papers, or documents related to the award; and will establish a proper accounting system in accordance with generally accepted accounting standards or agency directives.

3. Will establish safeguards to prohibit employees from using their positions for a purpose that constitutes or presents the appearance of personal or organizational conflict of interest, or personal gain.

4. Will initiate and complete the work within the applicable time frame after receipt of approval of the awarding agency.

5. Will comply with the Intergovernmental Personnel Act of 1970 (42 U.S.C. 4728-4763) relating to prescribed standards for merit systems for programs funded under one of the 19 statutes or regulations specified in Appendix A of OPM's Standards for a Merit System of Personnel Administration (5 C.F.R. 900, Subpart F).

6. Will comply with all Federal statutes relating to nondiscrimination. These include but are not limited to: (a) Title VI of the Civil Rights Act of 1964 (P.L. 88-352) which prohibits discrimination on the basis of race, color or national origin; (b) Title IX of the Education Amendments of 1972, as amended (20 U.S.C. 1681-1683, and 1685-1686), which prohibits discrimination on the basis of sex; (c) Section 504 of the Rehabilitation Act of 1973, as amended (29 U.S.C. 794), which prohibits discrimination on the basis of handicaps; (d) the Age Discrimination Act of 1975, as amended (42 U.S.C. 6101-6107), which prohibits discrimination on the basis of age; (e) the Drug Abuse Office and Treatment Act of 1972 (P.L. 92-255), as amended, relating to nondiscrimination on the basis of drug abuse; (f) the Comprehensive Alcohol Abuse and Alcoholism Prevention, Treatment and Rehabilitation Act of 1970 (P.L. 91-616), as amended, relating to nondiscrimination on the basis of alcohol abuse or alcoholism; (g) 523 and 527 of the Public Health Service Act of 1912 (42 U.S.C. 290 dd-3 and 290 ee 3), as amended, relating to confidentiality of alcohol and drug abuse patient records; (h) Title VIII of the Civil Rights Act of 1968 (42 U.S.C. 3601 et seq.), as amended, relating to nondiscrimination in the sale, rental or financing of housing; (i) any other nondiscrimination provisions in the specific statute(s) under which application for Federal assistance is being made; and (j) the requirements of any other nondiscrimination statute(s) which may apply to the application.

7. Will comply, or has already complied, with the requirements of Titles II and III of the uniform Relocation Assistance and Real Property Acquisition Policies Act of 1970 (P.L. 91-646) which provide for fair and equitable treatment of persons displaced or whose property is acquired as a result of Federal or federally assisted programs. These requirements apply to all interests in real property acquired for project purposes regardless of Federal participation in purchases.

8. Will comply, as applicable, with the provisions of the Hatch Act (5 U.S.C. 1501-1508 and 7324-7328) which limit the political activities of employees whose principal employment

Previous Edition Usable

Authorized for Local Reproduction

Standard Form 424B (Rev. 7-97)
Prescribed by OMB Circular A-102

APPLICATION CHECKLIST

One original and four copies of the application are due by March 1, 1999!

A complete application must include:

☐ The *Application for Federal Assistance* (ED Form 424), completed according to the instructions and signed by an authorized official (page 1)

☐ The *Program Summary and Abstract* (page 2 - one page maximum)

☐ The *Table of Contents* (page 3)

☐ The *Program Narrative* (no more than 20 pages double-spaced)

☐ The *Budget* (ED Form 524) and brief *Budget Narrative*

☐ The required assurances, certifications and disclosure forms, including:
   - Assurances - Non-Construction Programs (Form OMB 424B)
   - The certification regarding lobbying; debarment, suspension and other responsibility matters; and drug-free workplace requirements (Form ED-80-0013)
   - The certification regarding debarment, suspension, ineligibility and voluntary exclusion-lower tier covered transactions (Form ED-80-0014)
   - Disclosure of lobbying activities (Form LLL)
   - If you are in a state that complies with Executive Order 12372, you must submit your application to the State Single Point of Contact and obtain clearance by May 20, 1999.

☐ The *Appendix*, providing only a list of consortium members or partners and letters of support or commitment; evidence of previous success (if applicable); and proposed steps to ensure equitable access and participation.

This form is for your own use and should not be submitted with your application!

Appendix 2
Scoring Rubric for the 21st Century Community Learning Centers Program

21st Century Community Learning Centers Program Application—Selection Criteria Reference Sheet

Selection Criteria

Each selection criterion is weighted with a point value. As a reviewer, you are responsible for using only the selection criteria to guide your evaluation of the applications. *Applicants have been asked to respond to the following selection criteria:*

1. Need for project *(30 points)*
(A) The extent to which the proposed project will provide services or otherwise address the needs of students at risk of educational failure.

Guide Questions for Reviewer
a) Does the applicant sufficiently describe how the services proposed will help meet the needs of the community?
b) Are any of the following factors included in the needs statement:
  • Poverty rates in the communities to be served?
  • Percentage and/or rapid growth of limited English proficient students and adults?
  • Percentage of Title I students?
  • Dropout and literacy rates and educational levels in the community?
c) Does the applicant make use of needs inventory to help determine the community needs and the gaps in available services?

2. Quality of Project Design *(30 points)*

(A) The extent to which the goals, objectives, and outcomes to be achieved by the proposed project are clearly specified and measurable.

(B) The extent to which the design of the proposed project is appropriate to and will successfully address the needs of the target population or other identified needs.

(C) The extent to which the proposed project will establish linkages with other appropriate agencies and organizations providing services to the target population.

Guide Questions for Reviewer

a) Does the description of activities provided by the applicant include the specific roles to be played by each of the partners and discuss anticipated results?

b) Does it appear that the activities can adequately address the central causes of the needs described by the applicant?

c) Does the applicant present realistic goals, objectives, and outcomes for the proposed activities that can be measured and quantified?

d) Are the roles of consortium members clearly defined and documentation provided to support their time and resource commitment to the project?

3. Adequacy of Resources *(15 points)*

A) The adequacy of support, including facilities, equipment, supplies, and other resources, from the applicant organization or the lead applicant organization.

B) The extent to which the costs are reasonable in relation to the number of persons to be served and to the anticipated results and benefits.

Guide Questions for Reviewer

a) Does the applicant clearly illustrate how resources and personnel will be allocated to the various project tasks and activities?

b) Does the applicant clearly explain how existing school resources and resources contributed by partners will be utilized to help carry out planned project activities?

c) Does the applicant provide documented evidence that the plans they propose have the support of those who authorized the activities, those who carry them out, and those who will be affected by the plans?

d) Does the applicant provided a detailed budget narrative that itemizes the requested support from the 21st CCLC Program and the resources to be obtained from other sources?

4. Quality of the Management Plan *(15 points)*

A) The adequacy of the management plan to achieve the objectives of the proposed project on time and within budget, including clearly defined responsibilities, timelines, and milestone for accomplishing project tasks.

B) How the applicant will ensure that a diversity of perspectives are brought to bear in the operation of the proposed project, including those parents, teachers, the business community, a variety of disciplinary and professional fields, recipients or beneficiaries of services, or others, as appropriate.

Guide Questions for Reviewer
a) Does the applicant use charts and timetables to help describe the structure of the project and the procedures for successful management?
b) Are the objectives, participants, events, beneficiaries, and anticipated results clearly spelled out?
c) Does the management structure appear adequate?
d) Is evidence provided that the applicant will seek guidance and advice from a variety of members of the community?

5. Quality of Project Evaluation *(10 points)*
A) The extent to which the methods of evaluation include the use of objective performance measures that are clearly related to the intended outcomes of the project and will produce quantitative and qualitative data to the extent possible.

Guide Questions for Reviewer
a) Does the applicant's plan include the program objectives and performance indicators established by the Government Performance and Results Act (GPRA) for the 21st CCLC Program? (the GPRA indicators are on pages 59 & 60 of the application)
b) Are benchmarks for monitoring progress towards specific objectives presented in a clear and concise manner?
c) Are measurable outcomes provided to assess impact on student learning and behavior?
d) Does the applicant identify the individual and/or organization that will serve as evaluator for the project and describe his/her qualifications?
e) Is the following information addressed in the evaluation design?
   - Types of data to be collected
   - Timetable for collecting various types of data
   - Design and methods (surveys, case studies, interviews, etc.) to be used in data collection process
   - Types of instruments to be developed and when
   - Procedures for how data will be analyzed
   - Availability of report on results and outcomes

6. Competitive Priority *(5 points)*
Projects designed to assist students to meet or exceed state and local standards in core academic subjects such as reading, mathematics, or science, as appropriate to the needs of the participating children.

Guide Questions for Reviewer
a) Does the applicant address how the project activities will help students meet or exceed standards?
b) Is particular attention given to helping students at risk of educational failure?

Appendix 3
Sample Cover Letter for Corporate or Foundation Grant

Sample Cover Letter

Letterhead Stationery

Date

Mr. Maury Moneybags, President
XYZ Foundation
7474 Main Street
Anytown, USA 85111

Dear Mr. Moneybags:

As Superintendent of the XYZ School District, I am pleased and excited about the enclosed grant application for the expansion of the ALLBRIGHT ACADEMICS PROGRAM at XYZ High School.

This unique program allows students to have contact with the same teachers for three (3) hours each day, thus enabling them to develop a close student-teacher relationship that is meaningful and significant. In addition, the program plans to incorporate cutting-edge technology into the curriculum by providing all students in the ALLBRIGHT ACADEMICS PROGRAM with a laptop computer to enable them to integrate the use of technology into their lives as working tools for productivity and organization and to involve their parents in the education process.

XYZ High School, an acclaimed Blue Ribbon Distinguished School, is the ideal target site for this highly innovative project. The staff is very competent and dedicated, the Principal is a respected leader in the school community, the parents are very supportive and the students are highly motivated. Unfortunately, at this time our budget will not allow for the full implementation of this worthy project. We are respectfully requesting that XYZ Foundation assist us by providing a grant in the amount of $144,856.

We feel that this project has positive implications for other schools and districts in this county and elsewhere. If funded, we would be pleased to publicize the grant to the community and welcome XYZ Foundation as an educational partner with the XYZ School District.

If you have any questions or concerns, please don't hesitate to contact me or the Principal of XYZ High School, Dr. Al Ready.

Thank your very much for your interest.

Sincerely,

Nancy Needsomemoney, Ph.D.
Superintendent

Encl: Grant Application

Appendix 4
A Sampling of K-12 Grant Winners

This appendix contains a sampling of recent K-12 grant winners. By studying the funding sources and going to their websites, you should be able to match up your needs with the funding agencies' priorities. Also, keep in mind that funding priorities change from time to time, so it is important to keep updated on a regular basis.

Compiled by:
eSchool News Online
Bethesda, Md
(www.eschoolnews.org/funding/awards.cfm)

(Reprinted with permission)

The following sampling of grant winners is presented to familiarize you with the many funding opportunities that are available to K-12 schools and school districts. This descriptive list has been gathered by eSchool News Online (*www.eschoolnews.org/funding/awards.cfm*) and is used with their permission. eSchool News Online is dedicated to providing the news, information, community, and services necessary to help school professionals improve education and leanring through the integration and application of technology.

This, along with other funding opportunities presented elsewhere in this book, can be used as a starting point for prospect research.

Grant Awards

Award Title: $30,000 from America Online

America Online, a wholly owned subsidiary of AOL Time Warner, has donated $30,000 to the University of Arizona to help it provide laboratories at Tuscon-area high schools to train students for careers in technology through Cisco Systems' Network Academy program. The funds will allow the University of Arizona to purchase Cisco training toolkits to be used at Pueblo High Magnet School, Cholla High Magnet School, and Tuscon High Magnet School, all of which are located in disadvantaged communities in the Tuscon area. The Cisco training toolkits are high-tech labs consisting of routers, switches, cables, and ports that normally retail for about $18,000 each. Through a discount agreement with Cisco, the Tuscon Unified School District was able to purchase each lab for $10,000. The AOL Technologies University Relations Program, which made the grant, seeks to build relationships with selected colleges and universities that support leading-edge technological research.

Contact: America Online

703-265-1746

N/A

http://www.aol.com

Award Title: $100,000 from the Sprint Foundation

The Sprint Foundation has donated $100,000 to Washington, DC, public schools for the creation of a new "technology high school" and an accompanying curriculum program at Ballou Senior High. The new technology-based high school will open at DC's McKinley High, which was closed three years ago and will reopen in the fall of 2002. The Technology High School at McKinley will use state-of-the-art teaching methods and technology to prepare high school students in Washington for the rigors of college study and the ever-changing workplace of the 21st century. "Sprint is proud to be the first company to make a donation of $100,000 to the development of the Technology High School at McKinley," said David P. Thomas, vice president of corporate relations and executive director of the Sprint Foundation. "The Sprint Foundation supports, as one of its key areas of focus, youth and educational initiatives," Thomas continued. "We're pleased to have this opportunity to advance education on a larger scale and look forward to helping create an environment that strives to provide students the best technology education available today."

Contact: Sprint Foundation

913-624-3343

N/A

http://www3.sprint.com/sprint/overview/commun.html

—————————————————

Award Title: $149,850 from the Sun Cobalt Foundation

The Sun Cobalt Foundation, a division of Sun Microsystems, recently announced a donation of 20 Qube server appliances to Lutheran schools throughout the United States. The equipment was donated to enhance students' access to the Internet and improve education. The Qube servers offer students email addresses, their own websites, and file storage space. The appliances let teachers administer students' Internet access and maintain a firewall through a browser of their choice. As Principal Perry Bresemann of St. Lorenz Lutheran School explained, "The application of the Qube for schools is tremendous. As a teaching tool, the Qube allows students to set up entire systems, test their systems, and make modifications." This most recent donation of 20 Qubes totaled $19,980. Sun Microsystems has donated 150 Qube appliances to schools in the past six months, amounting to a total of $149,850.

Contact: Sun Cobalt Foundation

415-222-9691

N/A

http://www.sun.com

—————————————————

Award Title: $500,000 from Toyota Motor Sales

Toyota Motor Sales U.S.A. awarded nearly $500,000 in Tapestry grants to 50 U.S. science teachers at the National Science Teachers Association (NSTA) annual convention. The largest K-12 science grant program in the country, Toyota Tapestry has awarded nearly $4.5 million in grants in 11 years, and many of the award-winning projects incorporate the use of technology. This year's winning projects include:

- A study of Montana's wildfires of 2000
- Alternative sources of energy—including plasma, retaining ponds, and soybeans
- Landscaping with low-water vegetation on Western Navajo Nation land
- An analysis of the impact of seatbelts using hand-crafted "crash dummies."

All Tapestry awardees received a free trip to St. Louis for the NSTA national convention, where they accepted their grants during a dinner reception.

Contact: Toyota Motor Sales

N/A

N/A

http://www.nsta.org/programs/tapestry

———————————

Award Title: $1.6 million from the Bill and Melinda Gates Foundation

Colorado became the latest U.S. state to receive a challenge grant to train school administrators in technology from the Bill and Melinda Gates Foundation. State officials announced that the $1.6 million grant would help support a two-year, $2.8 million program that will train Colorado educators to use technology in schools. "We want public and private schools in Colorado to advance from limited technology use to increased student achievement through the effective, widespread integration of technology throughout the state," Gov. Bill Owens said. School superintendents and principals will be trained first and then will work with educators in their districts to integrate technology into classroom lessons. The sessions will start this summer. The Gates Foundation offers State Challenge Grants for Leadership Development to consortia in each state. The grants aim to develop school leaders who are dedicated to using technology to improve student learning.

Contact: The Bill and Melinda Gates Foundation

206-709-3100

N/A

http://www.gatesfoundation.org

———————————

Award Title: Education Department awards new grant to Santana High School

On March 16, Education Secretary Rod Paige announced that the U.S. Department of Education (ED) would provide a $50,152.52 grant to the Grossmont Union High School District under Project School Emergency Response to Violence (Project SERV). Grossmont is the district that houses Santana High School in Santee, Calif. "In the aftermath of a school shooting, we need to give our students and their families important counseling and support services to help them to cope with the consequences," Paige said. He added that "school violence affects all parts of a local community, and this is one way (ED) can assist states and local school districts during times of crisis." The grant is the first of its kind under Project SERV, a new program created to provide financial assistance to local school districts that have experienced a traumatic event such as a school shooting. Project SERV makes funds available to those districts for use in connection with event response and the reestablishment of a safe environment that is conducive to learning. Project SERV was created with a $10 million appropriation from Congress last year. Guidelines for the program are still being developed, but draft guidelines for grants under the program recommend that ED make Project SERV funds available for short-term assistance to school districts, as well as to support longer-term crisis response needs. Project SERV is administered through ED's Safe and Drug Free Schools program. The Grossmont Union High School District will use the grant funds for security, counseling, support, and translation services to allow the district to assist Spanish-speaking families.

Contact: Safe and Drug-Free Schools Program: Project SERV

202-260-3954

safeschl@ed.gov

http://www.ed.gov/offices/OESE/SDFS/grants.html

———————————————

Award Title: $100,000 from the Weingart Foundation

A $100,000 grant from the Los Angeles-based Weingart Foundation will help California Institute of Technology (Caltech) researchers team up with Los Angeles-area high school students to study ultrahigh-energy cosmic rays on their own campuses, school officials announced Feb. 8.

The grant allows Caltech to establish the California High School Cosmic-Ray Observatory, or CHICOS, on four campuses in the Northridge area. The program eventually may be expanded to 50 and possibly hundreds of sites, school officials said.

"This grant will give many high school students a unique opportunity to participate in research science at the university level," said Caltech President David Baltimore. "It will serve as a model for future collaborations in other subjects between world-class research universities and high schools."

The program will incorporate a high-school teacher education component. Teachers will develop curriculum materials to help their students participate in research. Caltech also will host a summer workshop where physics teachers and students can participate in the construction of detector stations for deployment at additional sites.

The initial school sites will be at Sylmar, Van Nuys, and Harvard Westlake High Schools and Sherman Oaks Continuing Education School.

The project will involve development and construction of detector hardware, associated electronics, and computer equipment to form a network among the high schools.

A large array of this type will enable the study of ultrahigh-energy cosmic rays through the detection of "showers," several kilometers in radius, of secondary particles they create in the Earth's atmosphere. When a majority of the 50 sites are operating, officials expect the project to yield significant results that will be reported in scientific literature.

The Weingart Foundation makes grants to a wide range of human service organizations, educational and health institutions, and cultural centers throughout Southern California.

Contact: Weingart Foundation

(213) 688-7799

N/A

http://http://www.weingartfnd.org/w.grant.html

———————————————

Award Title: $300,000 from the NEC Foundation

NEC Foundation of America has announced grants totaling $300,000 to eight organizations that demonstrate a common focus on science and technology education, and/or the application of technology to assist people with disabilities. "Our grantees apply the power of technology and innovation to make things possible for so many individuals," noted Hisashi Kaneko, foundation president. "That is the legacy of (our) grants—focusing on projects that use technology to maximize individual potential."

Organizations receiving support from this recent round of grants include Chicago Academy of Sciences, $50,000 to support the continued expansion of a nationwide network of 100 classrooms (grades 7-12) in Total CAoS, a national model for integrating communication technologies—such as live web broadcasts—into science and math education; the Math Science Network of Oakland, CA, $15,000 to support improvements to the Expanding Your Horizons website (www.expandingyourhorizons.org) to better serve volunteer scientists participating in year-round support or mentoring for middle and high school girls across the United States; and the Network for Instructional TV Inc. of Reston, VA, $60,000 toward development of Effective Resources for Educators and Disabled Youth (E-READY), which will become a special education resource center on the TeachersFirst web site (www.teachersfirst.com).

NEC Foundation of America was established in 1991 and endowed at $10 million by NEC Corp. and its U.S. subsidiaries. Since its inception, the foundation has awarded grants totaling $3.9 million.

Contact: NEC Foundation of America

(631) 753-7021

http://www.nec.com/company/foundation

———————————————

Award Title: $1 million from 3Com Corp.

3Com Corp., in collaboration with the United States Conference of Mayors, awarded a total of $1 million in networking equipment and consulting services to 10 U.S. cities on Jan. 18. This is the second phase of the company's Urban Challenge program, which was created to help cities integrate technology into their communities, enhance education and public communications systems, and help close the digital divide.

Almost all of the 2001 Urban Challenge winners will use funds to improve access to technology in their cities' public schools. The city of Detroit, Detroit Public Schools, and 3Com are teaming up to provide internet access in their after-school programs through 3Com's Ethernet, wireless, and voice technologies, for example. And with its award, the Indianapolis Public Schools are providing an education framework for at-risk students by creating two new schools. 3Com will donate leading-edge data communications equipment to the city for these schools, allowing their students to receive mentorship from local businesses and community role models.

Other 2001 grant recipients are Atlanta; Fort Worth, TX; Minneapolis, MN; Oakland, CA; Philadelphia; Sandy City, UT; Troy, NY; and Vineland, NJ. These cities join 10 recipients of grants in 2000: Baltimore, MD; Charleston, SC; Chaska, MN; Chester, PA; Denver, CO; Glascow, KY; Madison, WI; New Orleans, LA; Pontiac, MI; and Providence, RI.

Contact: 3Com Corp.

http://www.3com.com/urbanchallenge

——————————————————

Award Title: $1.36 million from the Gates Foundation

The Bill and Melinda Gates Foundation has given $1.36 million to the Diocese of Yakima Catholic School District in Washington to recognize and encourage achievement and leadership in education.

La Salle High School in Yakima and seven elementary schools in Ephrata, Kennewick, Richland, Sunnyside, Wenatchee, and Yakima will benefit from the grant.

The grant, the 11th made to school districts in Washington by the Gates Foundation, was announced Jan. 31. The districts are selected based on their commitment to using research-based models for achievement; emphasizing professional development; improving access to technology; and building community and home partnerships.

"This grant award is truly a blessing," said Cathy Colver, diocesan superintendent of schools. "It will provide the schools with the professional assistance, staff development, and equipment needed to weave the use of technology into every aspect of their students' learning experience."

The seven elementary schools in the district are St. Rose of Lima in Ephrata, St. Joseph in Kennewick, Christ the King in Richland, St. Joseph in Sunnyside, St. Joseph in Wenatchee, St. Joseph/Marquette in Yakima, and St. Paul Cathedral in Yakima. The schools are open to any student, regardless of ability to pay or religious affiliation.

Contact: The Bill & Melinda Gates Foundation

http://www.gatesfoundation.org

————————————————

Award Title: $1 million from Microsoft Corp.

Microsoft Corp. announced it will donate $1 million to University of California at Los Angeles School Management Program for the implementation of a Connected Learning Community at the Laguna Nueva Elementary School in Commerce, CA. The grant will be used to purchase computers and software, set up Internet connections, and show teachers, students, and members of the community how to use the equipment for education and communication.

UCLA's School Management Program is developing a model school to illustrate a program that will improve student learning and increase the participation of families in their children's education, according to Dan Chernow, the program's executive director. "We are excited to be a part of this innovative new program to help students and parents cross the technology gap and learn to use technology to positively affect their lives," he said.

Funds for the Laguna Nueva Elementary School project come from Microsoft's antipiracy recovery efforts, reflecting the fact that the Los Angeles district attorney helped Microsoft recover nearly $10 million in counterfeit software and cash from a major counterfeiting ring in the area.

Microsoft estimates it will recoup approximately $25 million in the next five years through this program, and it has pledged to donate at least half these funds to supporting school technology ventures. In July 2000, Microsoft made its first corporate donation under this program, providing $300,000 to the Boys & Girls Club of Westminster, CA, to help it create a library and multimedia laboratory.

Generally, Microsoft's corporate philanthropy is focused on creating greater access to technology in disadvantaged communities in the United States and around the world.

Contact: Microsoft Corp.

http://www.microsoft.com/piracy

————————————————

Award Title: $167 million from the California Department of Education

Delivering on a promise to help bridge the digital divide in California classrooms, Governor Gray Davis on Jan. 18 announced the release of $167 million in education technology grants for the state's high schools.

More than 108,000 multimedia, Internet-capable computers will be added to high schools as a result of these grants, Davis said. The grants will bring the statewide ratio of students to multimedia computers down to 5 to 1 across the state. When older computers are factored in, the statewide ratio of total computers to students will be about 3.8 to 1, down from 7 to 1. Before these grants, some schools had ratios as poor as 24 to 1.

More than 1,800 high schools will receive grants under the program. About $4 million of the funds will purchase Internet wiring and computer hardware for students to access Advanced Placement courses online. The remaining $163 million will be used to purchase new computers.

The funds to purchase internet wiring and computer hardware for online Advanced Placement courses are part of the governor's commitment to bringing rigorous AP courses to more students. These funds will be awarded to 155 schools that have agreed to use the technology to offer students a total of four or more AP courses when school opens this fall.

The new technology funds are part of the education technology package sponsored by Davis and enacted as part of the 2000 state budget. In addition to the $167 million announced Jan. 18, another $8 million in technology grants will be awarded in the coming weeks, the governor said.

Contact: California Department of Education

http://www.ose.ca.gov/edtech

———————————————

Award Title: $36.9 million to California schools from the Gates Foundation

In November, the Bill and Melinda Gates Foundation announced commitments of $36.9 million to 64 small public schools in California that are creating personalized learning environments to help all students achieve. Recipients of the grants have demonstrated the ability to use technology as a learning tool, as well as involve parents in education and create collaborative environments, said Tom Vander Ark, executive director of the foundation's education initiatives.

"These grants will have a tremendous impact on education in our state," said Gov. Gray Davis in a ceremony to mark the announcement of the first five recipients. "I've seen first-hand the positive impact of High-Tech High in San Diego. I am particularly grateful these funds will, among other things, create 10 new high-tech high schools in California."

Grant recipients include:

- The New Technology Foundation (slightly more than $4.9 million) has developed the New Technology High School in Napa and will create 10 more schools in northern California based on that model. Its model school has a student-to-computer ratio of one-to-one and technology has been integrated throughout the curriculum. New schools will be sited in communities with strong political, industrial, and parental support.

- The High-Tech High Foundation received approximately $6.4 million. This southern California group will create 10 technology-focused schools on the model of the High-Tech High in San Diego. These schools immerse students in a rigorous learning environment that engages their interest in the fields of math, engineering, and science.

- The Bay Area Coalition of Small Schools has received approximately $15.7 million to create a network of 22 to 35 small public schools in the greater San Francisco-Oakland metropolitan area.

- Aspire Public Schools received nearly $3.2 million to open five small high schools in the next three years.
- National Council of La Raza received nearly $6.8 million to establish a network of at least 15 charter schools serving Latino communities throughout California.

Contact: N/A

http://www.gatesfoundation.org

————————————————

Award Title: $68 million from the Lilly Endowment

The Indianapolis-based Lilly Endowment has implemented the first year of a multi-year grant program to support "raising the education level of people of all ages" through numerous educational and community organizations in Indiana. Initiated in September 1999, the Community Alliances to Promote Education program is providing grants to support a range of projects related to youth and adult literacy, parental involvement in education, teacher development, use of technology, and education of at-risk children. Ten organizations statewide received a total of $68 million in 2001 to implement proposals they had developed with earlier planning grants of $50,000 each. "We were so pleased with the caliber of the proposals and impressed with the obvious community enthusiasm for them that we felt compelled to add to the resources ($50 million) we originally allocated," said Sara B. Cobb, the endowment's vice president for education.

Although the Lilly Endowment does not specifically require technology as a component of the Community Alliances program, endowment representative Gretchen Wolfram said many of the projects are using technology to achieve their aims. "We let the people in the field tell us what they need," she said. "We have found that many projects have technology as a major element even if, for example, the goal that they have set out is to improve the reading skills of second-graders."

Examples of recipients include:

- Switzerland County School Corp.—$5 million to improve high school science and technology education through distance learning programs with state-supported colleges and universities.
- Spencer-Own County Community School Corp.—$3 million to create the Owen County Learning Network, which will emphasize parental and community access to and involvement in pre-K to 12th grade education. An alternative school will be created for middle and high school students.

The endowment will make approximately $115 million in grants next year, some of which will be available for current recipients to expand their programs and some of which will go to applicants who were unsuccessful this year. "Those groups with planning grants that were not funded this year are encouraged to revise their programs," said Wolfram. "This is an ongoing program." The deadline for revisions to implementation grant requests or for new organizations to submit applications for $50,000 planning grants is March 16.

The Lilly Endowment has been a strong supporter of numerous ed-tech initiatives in Indiana. Last August, for example, the endowment provided about $133,000 to the Corporation for Educational Technology to help create a "virtual" high school, to be known as the Indiana Online Academy. At the same time, it made a grant of $272,000 to develop a web-based program that will enable teachers to test their own computer proficiency and help them set goals for improvement.

Contact: Gretchen Wolfram

(317) 916-7304

Award Title: $213 million from the U.S. Department of Education

U.S. Secretary of Education Richard W. Riley on Jan. 3 announced the award of nearly $213 million in new grants to 386 school districts in 46 states to establish high-quality, after-school community learning centers. Riley also opened a new $200 million competition that will provide after-school grants to an additional 400 communities this spring, and technology is one of the activities that is eligible for funding.

The grants announced Jan. 3 will support about 1,500 new school-based centers in communities across the country that have submitted well-developed plans for meeting the needs of young people in their communities. These centers, in collaboration with community partners, will provide enriched learning opportunities in a safe environment for 300,000 children and 100,000 adults outside of regular school hours and during the summer.

The new grants and competition are funded under $846 million recently appropriated by Congress for the 21st Century Community Learning Centers program. The appropriation also continues funding for 805 communities—serving approximately 650,000 youth and 200,000 adults—which started after-school programs during the past two years. The average grant award is nearly $500,000 and supports four centers.

"President Clinton asked Congress to significantly expand support for after-school programs that provide extra help and extended learning opportunities," Riley said, "and Congress has responded. This new $846 million investment in our children will provide them critical extra learning help in safe places after school and during the summer."

The 21st Century Community Learning Centers program helps schools stay open longer to provide youth tutoring and homework help, academic enrichment, college prep activities, enrichment through the arts (including chorus, band, and drama), technology education, drug and violence prevention counseling, supervised recreational opportunities, and services for youth with disabilities.

Contact: N/A

http://www.ed.gov/21stcclc

Award Title: $2 million to Pennsylvania schools from the Heinz Endowments

The Heinz Endowments will give K-12 schools in southwestern Pennsylvania $2 million to purchase software developed by Carnegie Learning Inc. to help children learn algebra. Carnegie's software is sold under the trade name Cognitive Tutor.

The grants will be made to the schools through the Math & Science Collaborative, a state-supported program in 11 counties. The collaborative will administer the program and help analyze the results. Schools seeking funds must agree to allow the Math & Science Collaborative to undertake some research about student performance, such as grades in Algebra I and scores on standardized national tests.

The Cognitive Tutor curriculum has been designated by the United States Department of Education as one of five "exemplary" curricula, and it is used by many school districts across the country. The software encourages interactive learning that will lead to better student motivation and better retention of information, according to executives at Carnegie Learning. For more information about the software, contact Jennifer Kelly at (412) 683-5030, ext. 111. For more information about the collaborative:

Contact: Marcia Seeley

412-201-7409.

http://www.carnegiesciencecenter.org/collab

Award Title: $110,000 to train new teachers in technology from Intel Corp.

Intel Corp. has awarded the University of New Mexico $110,000 as part of an international program aimed at training teachers to use computers in the classroom. Intel presented UNM's College of Education with the grant in December to help the school jump-start Intel's Teach the Future program, which will train 4,800 teachers in New Mexico in the next two years.

The program will begin at UNM in May. Teachers will be trained to integrate current generation computers and software into existing lesson plans, as well as create new lessons that directly involve computer-assisted tasks. College of Education Dean Viola Florez noted that schools have become immersed in computers and technology in the past several years, but staffs at those schools have had minimal training in the new technology.

Over the two-year span of the project, Intel is expected to donate nearly $1.5 million in cash, service, equipment, and training to UNM. Also, Microsoft has donated several thousand dollars worth of software for use in the program. In its first year, the program will teach and certify 100 New Mexico teachers who will be trained as "master teachers," said Smith Frederick, the project's coordinator. Master teachers will then be responsible for teaching at least 20 other teachers in their respective districts.

Contact: Intel Corp

http://www.intel.com

————————————————

Award Title: $323,000 from the Verizon Foundation

Urban school districts across upstate New York will benefit from a $323,000 grant from the Verizon Foundation for technology-based literacy programs. The gift was announced by New York Lt. Gov. Mary O. Donohue and representatives of the Verizon Foundation, the philanthropic arm of Verizon Communications. Verizon will provide the funds to Education 21, a nonprofit agency based in Troy. Education 21 will take applications from urban school districts and distribute the funds in the form of one-time grants. The funding is targeted at urban school districts, because they face the greatest challenge in meeting higher literacy standards and assessments, program officials said. The grants will be used to purchase equipment and technology to further literacy efforts by the school districts. The funds will pay for computers for students and high-speed Internet connections in classrooms and the homes of some inner-city students. "We have a long-standing commitment to support the use of technology to enhance educational programs," said Richard Amadon, director of community relations for Verizon in upstate New York. Besides the purchase of computers and high-speed Internet access, funding will be used to buy software designed to promote literacy programs, establish activities to support these programs, and support efforts to get parents more involved in their children's education. The Verizon Foundation supports programs that create innovative eSolutions, help bridge the digital divide, foster basic and computer literacy, and create a skilled workforce.

Contact: Cliff Lee of Verizon

(518) 396-1095

clifford.p.lee@verizon.com

http://www.verizon.com/foundation

————————————————

Award Title: $100,000 from Microsoft Corp.

In an effort to increase interest and proficiency in science, engineering, and technology among girls, Microsoft Corp. has donated $100,000 to the Society of Women Engineers to fund mentoring and education programs in K-12 schools. "Microsoft and other technology companies have a vested interest in increasing the number of women with math and science backgrounds, not only in response to the number of jobs open, but to foster a diverse and more effective workforce," said Deborah Willingham, vice president of human resources for Microsoft. "SWE is providing educators and youth leaders with the kinds of innovative, skill-building tools and curricula that will help them interest girls in technical subjects, leading eventually to more women pursuing technical careers." According to the Commission on the Advancement of Women and Minorities in Science, Engineering, and Technology Development, only 9 percent of today's jobs that require engineering backgrounds are filled with women. More women than men earn college degrees today, but women comprise less than 19 percent of engineering enrollment. SWE will use the Microsoft "Equal Access" grant to fund mentoring programs and science curricula that encourage girls from underrepresented racial or ethnic populations to study science or engineering through hands-on activities and web-based instruction. The Equal Access program was developed in conjunction with Microsoft's Community Affairs division as way to help fulfill the company's vision of providing access to technology and the Internet for everyone. Additional sponsors include Compaq Computer Corp., Hewlett-Packard Co., and VERITAS Software Corp.

Contact: Anne Perusek of the Society of Women Engineers

(216) 397-3315

anne.perusek@swe.org

http://www.swe.org

———————————————

Award Title: $3.2 million from America's Kids Connect

On Oct. 5 and 6, students, parents, and teachers from 28 states and 10 countries competed for $3.2 million in prizes in an online game show program, America's Kids Connect 2000. Overall, the winners represented 24 states and won 183 prizes. America's Kids Connect created the contest to increase awareness of the use of computers in schools and to generate parental and community participation in schools, said Chris Bates, the group's executive director. Some of the awards: International Assessment Network donated unlimited use of its MAPP program, which retails at $29 per user, to students in grades 9 to 12 throughout an entire state for a period of one year (Pennsylvania won the award). Training for teachers and guidance counselors in the state also is included. The MAPP program is an online tool that evaluates students' career interests and can assist students in planning their courses. Schools can use the tool in their school-to-work programs as well. James Integrated Technologies donated 100 WebClerk labs, which have a value of $21,000 each. These 20-station eCommerce labs include web servers, Quick Time training movies, and other tools to assist students in developing eCommerce businesses. Administrative support is provided, too. Edvenions donated two "Starship School" pilots worth $50,000 each. These are web communities designed for K-8 schools. Sun Microsystems donated two sets of five Sun Ray Internet appliances and server systems, each valued at $10,000. · Microsoft donated software and licenses for two 20-station computer labs, including Word, Excel, and Front Page. Altiris donated $30,000 in computer management software and licenses for schools. The next America's Kids Connect event is scheduled for Oct. 4, 2001.

Contact: America's Kids Connect

http://www.amkids.org

Award Title: $100,000 in tech support services for Minnesota schools

Nine Minnesota schools and districts are piloting a program aimed at reducing routine calls to computer help lines by 30 percent through services donated by Netven LLC of Austin, Texas, and KnowledgeBroker Inc. The companies value the services at nearly $100,000. Under the program, technical support personnel at selected schools and districts will receive complimentary access for the 2000-01 school year to Netven's PC-HMO web-based support tools, as well as the "Ask Me Online" web portal developed by KnowledgeBroker Inc., a leading provider of technical support content. Minnesota's Office of Technology, which developed the project and chose the grant recipients, believes the program will improve computer users' ability to get answers to routine questions without calling on overtaxed school district workers. Integrated Internet-based training and support will improve user and support staff abilities to operate the systems, said Paul Wasko, the state's manager of education technology initiatives. The grants are divided into three categories. District-wide grants are targeted toward school districts considering or actively providing centralized technical support for teachers and staff members. The other two grant programs directly engage students. In one, Cisco Academies will use PC-HMO and Ask Me Online to educate students as front-line help desk staff members. The tech-prep support development grant goes a step further, establishing an intensive training program for students in both technical and customer-service skills. When the program ends, schools can decide to continue the service at a predetermined cost.

Contact: Jim Schwartz, Minnesota Department of Administration

(651) 284-3351

Award Title: $4.8 million for New Jersey's Access-Collaboration-Equity program

New Jersey's State Board of Education has awarded 26 grants worth $4.8 million to help schools with large numbers of disadvantaged students to purchase computers, connect to the Internet, and educate students and parents about effective use of technology resources. The new program, known as Access-Collaboration-Equity (ACE), will make 24 more grants worth another $2.6 million in the next few months. The key to the program is developing after-school programs that will give students and parents access to computers they could not otherwise afford. "We know that most students who come from low-income households are unable to access and use a computer at home," said state Commissioner of Education David Hespe. "Through the ACE grants, school districts will be able to operate community centers for disadvantaged students and their families to use when school is not in session." ACE is funded through two federal grants—Goals 2000 and the Technology Literacy Challenge Fund—at up to $200,000 per grant recipient. Economically disadvantaged school districts serve as lead agencies for these grants and collaborate with community partners, businesses, municipalities, and statewide organizations to develop, staff, and plan activities at ACE centers. Each center will be staffed by qualified professionals after school and on weekends at public locations, including schools, libraries, community centers, or housing complexes, said state ED representative Rich Vespucci. Winning applicants proposed programs that would, among other activities, enable students to complete homework and develop classroom presentations, perform online research, communicate with experts elsewhere in the world, teach family members how to use technology, and work in groups on projects that support New Jersey's Core Curriculum Content Standards.

Contact: New Jersey's State Board of Education

http://www.state.nj.us/njded/techno/ace/abstract.htm

————————————————

Award Title: $5.9 million for Teacher Quality Enhancement grants

The U.S. Department of Education has awarded $5.9 million for eight new projects designed to better train teachers for the challenges of today's classrooms. "This program takes traditional teacher education off the campus and into the heart of the classroom and community," Secretary Richard Riley said. "These beginning-teacher grants are an added benefit for school districts that have trouble attracting and retaining teachers, especially secondary teachers with strong backgrounds in the subjects they teach." The grants support partnerships involving one or more college or university teacher preparation programs, university-level schools of arts and sciences, and a high-need K-12 school district. A K-12 district is considered "high need" if at least one of its elementary or secondary schools has 50 percent or more of its students from families with incomes below the poverty line, more than a third of its secondary teachers are not teaching in the content area in which they were trained to teach, or 15 percent or more of its teachers have left in the last three years. Among the program's four priorities is integrating technology in training, so beginning teachers can use technology effectively in the classroom. California State University at Northridge received nearly $240,000 this year (and nearly $1.2 million over five years) to work with the Los Angeles Unified School District to improve new teachers' ability to integrate their field experiences into the classroom and to show them how to use technology to improve student achievement in elementary schools. Another winner, Bowling Green State University, has been awarded nearly $790,000 this year (and $4,154,493 over five years) to work with several local organizations and the Toledo Public School District to create an interactive, web-based teacher professional development system.

Contact: The U.S. Department of Education

http://www.ed.gov/offices/OPE/heatqp

————————————————

Award Title: $3.6 million from the Lucent Technologies Foundation

The Lucent Technologies Foundation awarded $3.6 million to 11 partnerships between universities and public schools focused on improving K-12 education. The Lucent Technologies Foundation—the charitable arm of Lucent Technologies—will contribute about $50 million around the world this year toward youth development projects, including education.

The academic partnerships will receive either one- or three-year grants ranging from $90,000 to $450,000. Several have strong technology focuses, including:

- Connecticut College and New London Public Schools, for "Teach and Learn Partnership for Math and Science Excellence." This project received $91,000 to support a program that is designed to "blur the boundaries between K-12 and higher education in math and science," according to its developers. It builds on a current collaboration to expand a series of seminars for middle school teachers conducted by Connecticut College faculty in math, technology, and science. The program also enables middle school students to come to the college monthly to work with faculty on experiments in state-of-the-art laboratory space.

- Princeton University, Columbia University, Seton Hall University, Stevens Institute of Technology, Rutgers University at Camden, and New York University, for "The New York-New Jersey Partners in Science Program." This program has been funded with $106,000 this year and $395,000 cumulatively during the next three years to enable high school chemistry teachers to bring inquiry-based methodologies into their classrooms using cutting-edge technology. The program will help teachers develop new teaching strategies, foster long-term scholarly collaborations, and guide students toward careers in science. This funding expands a program established in 1988 in Arizona and later expanded in 1997 by the Camille and Henry Dreyfus Foundation.

In choosing grant recipients (66 proposals were submitted this year), the Lucent Foundation considers how programs address the following objectives: reform of urban schools; reform of professional development programs for teachers and teacher recognition programs; enhancement of curriculum in the areas of science and math to improve K-12 teaching and to increase excitement among students; and preparation of young people for an increasingly diverse world.

For information about future Lucent Technologies Foundation grants, contact the Philanthropic Initiative Inc. at (617) 338-2590.

Contact: Philanthropic Initiative Inc.

(617) 338-2590

Award Title: $56 million from the Bill and Melinda Gates Foundation

The latest education gift from the Bill and Melinda Gates Foundation supports programs that are developing innovative curricula for small K-12 schools, particularly schools that will use technology to a significant degree. The grants, which total $56 million, include the first Gates Foundation grants outside the state of Washington as part of the foundation's plan to support model programs across the country.

The Gates Foundation seeks programs that emphasize small classes and the use of technology, because the foundation's leaders believe that a small, personalized learning environment is the key to helping every student succeed. To qualify for consideration, the proposed and existing programs had to enroll fewer than 400 students, include the use of technology, create learning opportunities such as internships for every student, and connect each student with an adult mentor.

Several of the grants were directed at programs in Rhode Island and Massachusetts, one of which is being created by the Harvard Graduate School of Education. Another Massachusetts organization, the Center for Collaborative Education, was awarded $4.9 million to create the New England Center for Small Schools, which will open as many as 20 new small schools in the next five years. It also will provide evaluation and assessment support to help small schools strengthen student achievement and accountability.

The Gates Foundation continued to direct funds to the state of Washington, too. The University of Washington will receive $6.5 million, most of which ($5.8 million) will be used to fund the initial work of the Institute for K-12 Leadership, which was created earlier this year. The Institute will spend the next four years working to create model school programs in San Francisco, CA; Compton, CA, near Los Angeles, CA; Kansas City, MO; East St. Louis, IL; Detroit; Cincinnati, OH; Cleveland, OH; and Boston, MA. The remainder of the University of Washington funds will establish the Small Schools Program at the university's Center on Reinventing Public Education.

Contact: The Bill and Melinda Gates Foundation

(206) 709-3100

http://www.gatesfoundation.org

———————————————

Award Title: Hundreds of new computers from Oracle Corp.

Oracle Corp. is spearheading an effort to get inexpensive, Internet-ready computers into urban Chicago classrooms by the start of the school year through a partnership with the New Internet Computer Co., which was cofounded by Oracle chief executive Larry Ellison.

The company is built on the premise that computers dedicated to Internet browsing and email can be manufactured inexpensively and provide rapid access to online services for the millions of Americans who cannot afford conventional computers. New Internet Computers (NICs), which do not have internal memory, cost as little as $199.

Five hundred NICs, the flagship product of the New Internet Computer Co., already have been donated by Oracle to Chicago schools, and the company has pledged to match donations from area businesses to fund up to 500 additional units.

NICs are part of Ellison's plan to give all school children access to the Internet, a project called Oracle's Promise. In May, the program made its first donation of 1,200 NICs to the Dallas Independent School District, a commitment that ultimately will reach $100 million, according to Ellison.

Contact: Michael Salort

(646) 245-3588

http://www.thinknic.com

Award Title: Language learning system from Sony Electronics

Sony Electronics Inc. has selected Robert Service High School in Anchorage, AK, as the winner of its second annual Sony Symphony Grant Program. Sony will provide the school with its latest language-learning software, the Symphony LLC-8000A, and pay for training to use the system.

The Symphony educational package is a multimedia system that incorporates audio and visual components. The grant to Robert Service High School includes 10 digital PC recorders, an instructor console, and Windows-compatible software.

With the system, teachers can monitor students' language progress closely, said Ron Remschel, national sales and marketing manager for Sony Education Systems.

Contact: Sony Electronics Inc.

http://www.sel.sony.com/SEL/corpcomm/news/bandp/658.html

Award Title: Math and science technology training from Packard BioScience

This summer, Packard BioScience Co. treated K-12 teachers in Connecticut to a several-day course in using sophisticated electronic calculators in high school math and science classrooms. The program was part of the Project to Increase Mastery of Mathematics and Science (PIMMS), a series of professional development courses that provide state-of-the-art training and equipment to high school educators.

PIMMS programs strengthen and update teachers' command of subject matter, familiarize them with effective teaching strategies and practices, and guide them to serve as agents of change through workshops and other in-service activities. More than 600 teachers have completed multi-week training sessions and earned the title of PIMMS Fellow, and these fellows, in turn, have worked with an estimated 22,000 of their colleagues throughout the state.

In the program supported by Packard BioScience this year, high school teachers were trained to use TI-83 calculators developed and manufactured by Texas Instruments.

Contact: Packard BioScience Co.

http://www.wesleyan.edu/pimms

————————————————

Award Title: $500,000 from the Bell Atlantic Foundation

In June, the Bell Atlantic Foundation presented $500,000 to 19 projects in Massachusetts under its EdLink program. This is the last year of the program in its current format, because Bell Atlantic and GTE merged to become Verizon on June 30. The new company has started the Verizon Foundation.

The four-year-old EdLink program brings hands-on use of technology to students in ways that will help them develop a school-to-career focus. The grants target grades 7-12 in public and private school districts that collaborate with institutions of higher education, community organizations, nonprofit agencies, or businesses.

As an example of a 2000 grant winner, Northern Essex Community College will create an internship and distance-learning program that will provide 20 educators with multimedia training and models for the use of mathematics in real-world applications that will help them prepare their students for statewide math exams.

Contact: Bell Atlantic Foundation

http://foundation.verizon.com/edlink/

Glossary of Government Grants

Administrative regulations. Regulations that implement (1) guidance from OMB contained in circulars that apply to the administration of all federal grants and cooperative agreements, (2) Presidential Executive Orders (where regulation is necessary), and (3) legislation that affects all applicants for or recipients of federal grants and cooperative agreements; see also *EDGAR* (defined below).

Application Control Center. The administrative unit of the Department of Education (in the Office of the Chief Financial and Chief Information Officer (defined below)) that is officially authorized to receive applications for discretionary grants and cooperative agreements.

Application for Federal Education Assistance or ED 424. The grant application form, sometimes referred to as the application cover page, used by the Department of Education, beginning in 1998. This form replaces the SF 424, formerly used by the Department.

Application notice. A notice published in the *Federal Register* (defined below) that invites applications for one or more discretionary grant or cooperative agreement competitions, gives basic program and fiscal information on each competition, informs potential applicants when and where they can obtain applications, and cites the deadline date (defined below), for a particular competition.

Application package. A package that contains the application notice for one or more programs and all the information and forms needed to apply for a discretionary grant or cooperative agreement.

Appropriations legislation. A law passed by the Congress to provide a certain level of funding for a grant program in a given year.

Assurances. A listing of a variety of requirements, found in different federal laws, regulations, and executive orders, that applicants agree in writing to observe as a condition of receiving federal assistance.

Audit finding. A conclusion about a monetary or nonmonetary matter related to an auditor's examination of an organization, program, activity,

Reprinted with permission from *What Should I Know about Ed Grants?* U.S. Department of Education, Washington, DC 1998.

or function that frequently identifies problems and provides recommendations for corrective action in order to prevent their future recurrence.

Audit resolution process. The process by which the Department determines whether costs in an audit report are actually allowable or unallowable. If costs are identified as being unallowable, the Department initiates action to have grantee return unallowable expenditures.

Audit Resolution Specialist. The Department staff member who reviews audit reports of grantees and develops the proposed recommendations for settling cases of expenditures not allowed under discretionary grants or cooperative agreements. The recommendations become the basis for decisions issued in the Program Determination Letter (defined below).

Authorizing legislation. A law passed by the Congress that establishes or continues a grant program.

Budget period. An interval of time into which a project period is divided for budgetary purposes, usually twelve months.

Catalog of Federal Domestic Assistance. Publication and database produced by the General Services Administration that lists the domestic assistance programs of all federal agencies and gives information about a program's authorization, fiscal details, accomplishments, regulations, guidelines, eligibility requirements, information contacts, and application and award process; also called the CFDA.

Certification. A statement, signed by an applicant or grantee as a prerequisite for receiving federal funds, that it (1) meets or will adhere to certain conditions and/or (2) will undertake or not undertake certain actions.

CFDA number. Identifying number for a federal assistance program, composed of a unique two-digit prefix to identify the federal agency (>84 = for the Department of Education), followed by a period and a unique three-digit code for each authorized program.

Clarification contact. Contact with an applicant by a grant team member before the Department makes a funding decision in order to obtain more detailed information about programmatic and/or budgetary items in an application.

Code of Federal Regulation (CFR). Compilation of all final regulations issued by the National Archives and Records Administration; divided into numbered "Titles"; Title 34 contains the regulations of the Department of Education.

Combined Application Notice (CAN). A notice published by the Department in the *Federal Register* that identifies programs and competitions under which the Secretary has invited, or plans to invite, applications for new awards for a particular fiscal year. The notice provides the actual or estimated information on the following: (1) the date the competition will be announced in the *Federal Register*, (2) the date application packages will be available, (3) the application deadline date, (4) the deadline for Intergovernmental Reviews, (5) the range of awards, (6) the average size of awards, and (7) the number of awards. The CAN also provides a contact name and phone number to get further information.

Competitive review process. The process used by the Department of Education to select discretionary grant and cooperative agreement applications for funding in which applications are scored by subject-area experts and the most highly scored applications are considered for funding.

Continuation grant. Additional funding awarded for budget periods following the initial budget period of a multi-year discretionary grant or cooperative agreement.

Cooperative agreement. A type of federal assistance; essentially, a variation of a *discretionary grant* (defined below), awarded by the Department when it anticipates having substantial involvement with the grantee during the performance of a funded project.

Deadline date. The date by which an applicant must mail a discretionary grant or cooperative agreement application for it to be considered for funding by the Department. Under some competitions, the Department requires that the application be received by the deadline date.

Discretionary grant. An award of financial assistance in the form of money, or property in lieu of money, by the federal government to an eligible grantee, usually made on the basis of a competitive review process.

Discretionary Grant Team (Grant Team). A group of ED staff members in a program office responsible for all phases of the grants process including the review, award, administration, and closeout of discretionary grants. Grant teams work in partnership with grantees by providing guidance and technical assistance to ensure successful project outcomes.

ED. The acronym for the U.S. Department of Education (i.e., Education Department).

EDGAR (Education Department General Administrative Regulations). Administrative regulations governing the Department's discretionary grant and cooperative agreement programs found in Parts 74, 75, 76, 77, 79, 80, 81, 82, 85, and 86 of Title 34 of the CFR (defined above); a document issued by the Department that contains a reprint of these regulations.

Federal Register. A daily compilation of federal regulations and legal notices, presidential proclamations, executive orders, federal agency documents having general applicability and legal effect, documents required to be published by act of Congress, and other federal agency documents of public interest; prepared by the National Archives and Records Administration for public distribution by the Government Printing Office; Publication of record for ED regulations.

Financial Payments Group. The administrative unit of the Department if Education that makes payments of federal funds to grantees of discretionary grants and cooperative agreements.

Formula grant. A grant that the Department is directed by Congress to make to grantees, for which the amount is established by a formula based on certain criteria that are written into the legislation and program regulations; directly awarded and administered in the Department's program offices.

Funding offer. An instance when the Department proposes to a successful applicant, either orally or in writing, a level of funding less than the applicant request. Occurs when the Department either (1) does not accept certain items of cost in the applicant's original budget or (2) does not have a sufficient level of program appropriations to fund all recommended projects at the requested level.

Funding priorities. A means of focusing a competition on the areas in which the Secretary is particularly interested in receiving applications. Priorities take the form of specific kinds of activities that applicants are asked to include in an application. There are *Absolute Priorities*, which the applicant must address in order to be considered for funding; *Competitive Priorities*, which the applicant has the option of choosing whether to address and for which they may receive additional points, and; *Invitational Priorities*, which the applicant is encouraged but not required to address. Applications addressing invitational priorities receive no competitive or absolute preference over applications that do not meet the priority.

Grant Administration and Payment System (GAPS). A financial subsystem that is part of the Department's larger Education Central Automated Processing System (EDCAPS). GAPS provides online capabilities for grant recipients to request payments and access their account obtain their most current payment information.

Grant application reviewer (reviewer). An individual who serves the Department by reviewing new discretionary grant and cooperative agreement applications; also referred to as "field reader" or "peer reviewer."

Grantee. An individual or organization that has been awarded financial assistance under one of the Department's discretionary grant programs.

Grant Award Notification (GAN). Official document signed by the authorized official stating the amount and the terms and conditions of an award for a discretionary grant or cooperative agreement.

Grant closeout. The final step in the lifecycle of a discretionary grant or cooperative agreement. During this phase, the Department ensures that all applicable administrative actions are required work of the discretionary grant or cooperative agreement have been completed by the grantee. The Department also reconciles and/or makes any final fiscal adjustments to a grantee's account in GAPS.

Grant programs. For the purposes of this booklet, programs of discretionary grants and/or cooperative agreements administered by the Department of Education.

Grants Policy and Oversight Staff (GPOS). A component within the Office of the Chief Financial and Chief Information Officer responsible for policy development and oversight of the grants process at the Department. GPOS provides technical assistance to the program offices regarding discretionary grant planning, award, administration, and closeout; also responsible for maintaining *EDGAR*.

Indirect costs. Costs of an organization incurred for common or joint objectives that cannot be readily and specifically identified with a particular grant project or other institutional activity.

Indirect cost rate. A percentage established by a federal department or agency for a grantee organization that the grantee uses in computing the dollar amount it charges to the grant to reimburse itself for indirect costs incurred in doing the work of the grant project.

Monitoring. Activities undertaken by ED staff members to review and evaluate specific aspects of a grantee's activities under a discretionary grant or cooperative agreement; they include (1) measuring a grantee's performance, (2) assessing a grantee's adherence to applicable laws, regulations, and the terms and conditions of the award, (3) providing technical assistance to grantees, and (4) assessing whether a grantee has made substantial progress.

Notice of proposed rulemaking. An announcement published in the *Federal Register* of proposed new regulations or modifications to existing regulations; the first stage in the process of creating or modifying regulations.

Obligation. An entry made by a member of a discretionary grant team in the Department's automated accounting system that authorizes the Financial Payments Group to make payments of federal grant funds to a grantee.

Office of the Chief Financial and Chief Information Officer. An organizational unit in the Department whose primary responsibility is serving as a principal advisor to the Secretary of Education on all matters related to discretionary grant making, cooperative agreements, and procurement, as well as financial management, financial control, and accounting.

Office of Management and Budget (OMB). A branch of the Executive Office of the President. OMB helps the president formulate spending plans; evaluates the effectiveness of agency programs, policies, and procedures; assesses competing funding demands among agencies; and sets funding priorities. OMB ensures that agency reports, rules, testimony, and proposed legislation are consistent with the president's budget and with administration policies. In addition, OMB oversees and coordinates the administration's procurement, financial management, information, and regulatory policies. In each of these areas, OMB's role is to help improve administrative management, to develop better performance measures and coordinating mechanisms, and to reduce any unnecessary burdens on the public.

OMB circulars. Administrative policy documents issued by OMB that give instruction to federal agencies on a variety of topics, including the administration of federal grants and cooperative agreements.

Performance report. A report of the specific activities the recipient of a discretionary grant or cooperative agreement has performed during the budget or project period.

Post-award performance conference. The first major discussion between the Department and some grantees after a new award has been made. The conference generally focuses on the proposed project outcomes as stated in the grantee's approved application, and on the ways in which project progress will be assessed.

Principal office. For the purposes of this booklet, one of six organizational units of the Department responsible for administering programs that award discretionary grants and cooperative agreements: Office of Bilingual Education and Minority Languages Affairs (OBEMLA); Office of Educational Research and Improvement (OERI); Office of Elementary and Secondary Education (OESE); Office of Postsecondary Education (OPE); Office of Special Education and Rehabilitative Services (OSERS); and Office of Vocational and Adult Education (OVAE).

Principal Officer. The Department official who is head of one of the six Principal Offices listed above; holds the rank of assistant secretary or its equivalent.

Program Determination Letter (PDL). An official written notice from an authorized Department of Education management official to an audited grantee that sets forth the Department's decision on findings in an audit report, including all necessary actions and repayment of funds for which the grantee is responsible.

Program Office. A subunit of a Principal Office that conducts the daily work of administering the Department's discretionary grant and cooperative agreement programs, including the review and ranking of applications.

Program regulations. Regulations that implement legislation passed by Congress to authorize a specific grant program; they include applicant and participant eligibility criteria, nature of activities funded, allowability of certain costs, selection criteria under which applications will be selected for funding, and other relevant information.

Project period. The total amount of time (sometimes several years) during which the Department authorizes a grantee to complete the approved work of the project described in the application; project periods of more than one year are divided into budget periods. Sometimes referred to as "performance period."

PR/Award number. The identifying number for a discretionary grant or cooperative agreement award, composed of seven parts (e.g., H029A951234-95C):

1. Principal Office designator (H)
2. CFDA numeric suffix of the program (029)
3. Alphabetic subprogram identifier (A)
4. Last digit of the fiscal year of the competition (95)
5. Unique application identifier (1234)
6. Fiscal year of the funding (95)
7. Sequential order of the most recent funding action in a fiscal year (C)

The first five parts remain the same throughout the life of the project period while the last two parts change by budget period.

Regulations. For purposes of this booklet, federal rules of general applicability that are authorized by federal laws or other federal authority and contained in the CFR.

Student financial assistance. ED funding in support of undergraduate or graduate students attending colleges, universities, and other postsecondary institutions that meet the Department's eligibility requirements; provided by Student Financial Assistance Programs in the Department's Office of Postsecondary Education and administered separately from the Department's discretionary grant and cooperative agreement programs; sometimes referred to as "student aid."

Substantial progress. A level of achievement that a grantee must make in its project during a specified period of time (e.g., budget period, performance period), which produces measurable and verifiable evidence that the activities undertaken have attained a preponderance of project goals and objectives during the period.

Glossary of Corporate and Foundation Grants

Annual report. A voluntary report issued by a foundation or corporation that provides financial data and descriptions of its grantmaking activities. Annual reports vary in format from simple typewritten documents listing the year's grants to detailed publications that provide substantial information about the grantmaker's grantmaking programs.

Assets. The amount of capital or principal—money, stocks, bonds, real estate, or other resources—controlled by a foundation or corporate giving program. Generally, assets are invested and the resulting income is used to make grants.

Associates program. A fee-based membership program of the Foundation Center providing toll-free telephone reference, photocopy and fax service, and computer searches of Foundation Center databases.

Beneficiary. In philanthropic terms, the donee or grantee receiving funds from a foundation or corporate giving program is the beneficiary, although society benefits as well.

Capital support. Funds provided for endowment purposes, building, construction, or equipment.

CD-ROM. Acronym for Compact Disk-Read Only Memory. CD-ROMs are high capacity computer disks that allow publishers and other information providers to distribute large amounts of information in a searchable format.

Challenge grant. A grant that is paid only if the donee organization is able to raise additional funds from other sources. Challenge grants are often used to stimulate giving from other donors. See also *matching grant.*

Community foundation. A 501(c)(3) organization that makes grants for charitable purposes in a specific community or region. The funds available to a community foundation are usually derived from many donors and held in an endowment that is independently administered; income earned by the endowment is then used to make grants. Although a community foundation may be classified by the IRS as a private foundation, most are classified as public charities and are eligible for maximum

Reprinted with permission from *The Foundation Center's User-Friendly Guide to Funding Research & Resources,* 2001, Foundation Center, New York, NY.

tax-deductible contributions from the general public. See also *501(c)(3); public charity*.

Community fund. An organized community program that makes annual appeals to the general public for funds that are usually not retained in an endowment but are instead used for the ongoing operational support of local agencies. See also *federated giving program*.

Company-sponsored foundation (also referred to as a corporate foundation). A private foundation whose assets are derived primarily from the contributions of a for-profit business. While a company-sponsored foundation may maintain close ties with its parent company, it is an independent organization with its own endowment and as such is subject to the same rules and regulations as other private foundations. See also *private foundation*.

Cooperating Collection. A member of the Foundation Center's network of libraries, community foundations, and other nonprofit agencies that provides a core collection of Center publications in addition to a variety of supplementary materials and services in areas useful to grantseekers.

Corporate foundation. See *company-sponsored foundation*.

Cooperative venture. A joint effort between or among two or more grantmakers. Cooperative venture partners may share in funding responsibilities or contribute information and technical resources.

Corporate giving program. A grantmaking program established and administered within a for-profit corporation. Because corporate giving programs do not have separate endowments, their annual grant totals generally are directly related to company profits. Corporate giving programs are not subject to the same reporting requirements as corporate foundations.

DIALOG. An online database information service made available by Knight Ridder Information Services, Inc. The Foundation Center offers two large files on foundations and grants through DIALOG.

Distribution committee. The committee responsible for making grant decisions. For community foundations, the distribution committee is intended to be broadly representative of the community served by the foundation.

Donee. The recipient of a grant. Also known as the "grantee" or the "beneficiary."

Donor. An individual or organization that makes a grant or contribution to a donee. Also known as the "grantor."

Employee matching grant. A contribution to a charitable organization by an employee that is matched by a similar contribution from his or her employer. Many corporations have employee matching-gift programs in higher education that encourage their employees to give to the college or university of their choice.

Endowment. Funds intended to be invested in perpetuity to provide income for continued support of a not-for-profit organization.

Expenditure responsibility. In general, when a private foundation makes a grant to an organization that is not classified by the IRS as a "public charity," the foundation is required by law to provide some assurance that the funds will be used for the intended charitable purposes. Special reports on such grants must be filed with the IRS. Most grantee organizations are public charities and many foundations do not make "expenditure responsibility" grant.

Family foundation. An independent private foundation whose funds are derived from members of a single family. Family members often serve as officers or board members of family foundations and have a significant role in their grantmaking decisions. See also *operating foundation; private foundation; public charity.*

Federated giving program. A joint fundraising effort usually administered by a nonprofit "umbrella" organization that in turn distributes the contributed funds to several nonprofit agencies. United Way and community chests or funds, the United Jewish Appeal and other religious appeals, the United Negro College Fund, and joint arts councils are examples of federated giving programs. See also *community fund.*

Field office. The Washington, DC, Atlanta, Cleveland, and San Francisco reference collections operated by the Foundation Center, all of which offer a wide variety of service and comprehensive collections of information on foundations and grants.

501(c)(3). The section of the tax code that defines nonprofit, charitable (as broadly defined), tax-exempt organizations; 501(c)(3) organizations are further defined as public charities, private operating foundations, and private nonoperating foundations. See also *operating foundation; private foundation; public charity.*

Form 990-PF. The public record information return that all private foundations are required by law to submit annually to the Internal Revenue Service.

General/operating support. A grant made to further the general purpose or work of an organization, rather than for a specific purpose or project; also called an unrestricted grant.

General purpose foundation. An independent private foundation that awards grants in many different field of interest. See also *special purpose foundation.*

Grantee financial report. A report detailing how grant funds were used by an organization. Many corporate grantmakers require this kind of report from grantees. A financial report generally includes a listing of all expenditures from grant funds as well as an overall organizational financial report covering revenue and expenses, assets and liabilities.

Grassroots fundraising. Efforts to raise money from individuals or groups from the local community on a broad basis. Usually an organization's own constituents—people who live in the neighborhood served or clients of the agency's services—are the sources of these funds. Grassroots fundraising activities include membership drives, raffles, auctions, benefits, and a range of other activities.

Guidelines. Procedures set forth by a funder that grantseekers should follow when approaching a grantmaker.

Independent foundation. A grantmaking organization usually classified by the IRS as a private foundation. Independent foundations may also be known as family foundations, general purpose foundations, special purpose foundations, or private nonoperating foundations. The Foundation Center places independent foundations and company-sponsored foundations in separate categories; however, federal law normally classifies both as private, nonoperating foundations subject to the same rules and requirements. See also *private foundation*.

In-kind contribution. A contribution of equipment, supplies, or other tangible resource, as distinguished from a monetary grant. Some organizations may also donate the use of space or staff time as an in-kind contribution.

Matching grant. A grant that is made to match funds provided by another donor. See also *challenge grant; employee matching gift*.

Microfiche. Flat strips of microfilm. The Foundation Center collects and make available foundation 990-PFs on microfiche mounted on aperture cards by the IRS.

Operating foundation. A 501(c)(3) organization classified by the IRS as a private foundation whose primary purpose is to conduct research, social welfare, or other programs determined by its governing body or establishment charter. An operating foundation may make grants, but the sum generally is small relative to the funds used for the foundation's own program. See also *510(c)(3)*.

Operating support grant. A grant to cover the regular personnel, administrative, and miscellaneous expenses of an existing program or project. See also *general/operating support*.

Orientation. An introduction to available resources and fundraising research strategies presented by Foundation Center library staff. Supervisors at Cooperating Collections may conduct orientation sessions as well.

Payout requirement. The minimum amount that private foundations are required to expend for charitable purposes (including grants and, within certain limits, the administrative cost of making grants). In general, a private foundation must meet or exceed an annual payout requirement of 5 percent of the average market value of it total assets.

Private foundation. A nongovernmental, nonprofit organization with funds (usually from a single source, such as an individual, family, or corporation) and program managed by its own trustees or directors. Private foundations are established to maintain or aid social, educational, religious, or other charitable activities serving the common welfare, primarily through the making of grants. See also *501(c)(3); public charity*.

Program amount. Funds that are expended to support a particular program administered internally by a foundation or corporate giving program.

Program officer. A staff member of a foundation who reviews grant proposals and processes applications for the board of trustees. Only a small percentage of foundations have program officers.

Program-related investment (PRI). A loan or other investment (as distinguished from a grant) made by a foundation to another organization for a project related to the foundation's philanthropic purposes and interests.

Proposal. A written application, often accompanied by supporting documents, submitted to a foundation or corporate giving program in requesting a grant. Most foundations and corporations do not use printed application forms but instead require written proposals; other prefer preliminary letters of inquiry prior to a formal proposal. Consult published guidelines.

Public charity. A nonprofit organization that qualifies for tax-exempt status under section 501(c)(3) of the IRS code. Public charities are the recipients of most foundation and corporate grants. Some public charities also make grants. See also *501(c)(3); private foundation.*

Qualifying distributions. Expenditures of a private foundation made to satisfy its annual payout requirement. These can include grants, reasonable administrative expenses, set-asides, loans and program-related investments, and amounts paid to acquire assets used directly in carrying out tax-exempt purposes.

Query letter. A brief letter outlining an organization's activities and its request for funding that is sent to a potential grantmaker in order to determine whether it would be appropriate to submit a full grant proposal. Many grantmakers prefer to be contacted in this way before receiving a full proposal.

RFP. An acronym for Request for Proposal. When the government issues a new contract or grant program, it sends out RFPs to agencies that might be qualified to participate. The RFP lists project specifications and application procedures. While a few foundations occasionally use RFPs in specific fields, most prefer to consider proposals that are initiated by applicants.

Seed money. A grant or contribution used to start a new project or organization. Seed grants may cover salaries and other operating expenses of a new project.

Set-asides. Funds set aside by a foundation for a specific purpose or project that are counted as qualifying distributions toward the foundation's annual payout requirement. Amounts for the project must be paid within five years of the first set-aside.

Special purpose foundation. A private foundation that focuses it grantmaking activities in one or a few areas of interest. See also *general purpose foundation.*

Sponsorship. Affiliation with an existing nonprofit organization for the purpose of receiving grants. Grantseekers may either apply for federal tax-exempt status or affiliate with a nonprofit sponsor.

Tax-exempt. Refers to organizations that do not have to pay taxes such as federal or state corporate tax or state sales tax. Individuals who make donations to such organizations may be able to deduct these contributions from their income tax.

Technical assistance. Operational or management assistance given to nonprofit organizations. It can include fundraising assistance, budgeting and financial planning, program planning, legal advice, marketing, and other aids to management. Assistance may be offered directly by the staff of a foundation or corporation, or it may be provided in the form of a grant to pay for the services of an outside consultant. See also *in-kind contributions.*

Trustee. A foundation board member or officer who helps make decisions about how grant monies are spent. Depending on whether the foundation has paid staff, trustees may take a more or less active role in running its affairs.

Index